SECOND EDITION

INTERACTIONS I
A Writing Process Book

Margaret Keenan Segal

Development Center for Afghan Education

Cheryl Pavlik

Oman Ministry of Education

With contributions by Laurie Blass

McGraw-Hill, Inc.

New York St. Louis San Francisco Auckland Bogotá
Caracas Lisbon London Madrid Mexico Milan
Montreal New Delhi Paris San Juan Singapore
Sydney Tokyo Toronto

This is an EBI book

Interactions I
A Writing Process Book
Second Edition

5 6 7 8 9 0   DOC/DOC   9 9 8 7 6 5 4 3 2

ISBN 0-07-557526-4

Manufactured in the United States of America

Sponsoring editor: Eirik Børve
Developmental editor: Mary McVey Gill
Project editor: Marie Deer
Copyeditor: Pat Campbell
Art director: Jamie Sue Brooks
Text and cover designer: Cheryl Carrington
Cover illustration: Rufino Tamayo: *Wedding Portrait (Retrato matrimo-
nial),* 1967. Oil on canvas, 136 × 195 cm. B. Lewin Galleries/Palm
Springs, California.
Illustrators: Axelle Fortier and Sally Richardson
Typesetting: Graphic Typesetting Service
R. R. Donnelley & Sons Company was printer and binder.

CONTENTS

Chapter 7   HEALTH AND ILLNESS   78

Chapter 8   TELEVISION AND THE MEDIA   92

Chapter 9   FRIENDS AND SOCIAL LIFE   104

Rhetorical focus: biographical narration
Grammatical and stylistic focus: present perfect and
present perfect continuous tenses with *for* and *since;*
contrast of verb tenses; using *in fact*

Chapter 10   CUSTOMS, CELEBRATIONS, AND HOLIDAYS   118

Rhetorical focus: classification
Grammatical and stylistic focus: gerunds and infinitives;
using *in addition to, besides, another,* and *the first,*
second, third, last; pronouns; quantifiers;
nonrestrictive relative clauses

Chapter 11   RECREATION   132

Rhetorical focus: persuasion
Grammatical and stylistic focus: present perfect and present perfect continuous tenses; pronouns; gerunds

Chapter 12   YOU, THE CONSUMER   146

Rhetorical focus: writing a formal letter of complaint
Grammatical and stylistic focus: contrast of verb tenses; using past participles as adjectives

PREFACE
to the Second Edition

To the Instructor

INTERACTIONS: THE PROGRAM

Interactions consists of ten texts plus two instructor's manuals for in-college or college-bound nonnative English students. *Interactions I* is for high-beginning to low-intermediate students, while *Interactions II* is for low-intermediate to intermediate students. Within each level, I and II, the books are carefully coordinated by theme, vocabulary, grammar structure, and, where possible, language functions. A chapter in one book corresponds to and reinforces material taught in the same chapter of the other three books at that level for a truly integrated, four-skills approach.

Each level, I and II, consists of five books plus an instructor's manual. In addition to *A Writing Process Book,* they include:

A Communicative Grammar I, II: Organized around grammatical topics, these books include notional/functional material where appropriate. They present all grammar in context and contain a wide variety of communicative activities.

A Reading Skills Book I, II: The selections in these books are written by the authors and carefully graded in level of difficulty and amount of vocabulary. They include many vocabulary-building exercises and emphasize reading strategies: for example, skimming, scanning, guessing meaning from context, understanding the structure and organization of a selection, increasing reading speed, and interpreting the author's point of view.

A Listening/Speaking Skills Book I, II: These books use lively, natural language from a variety of contexts—dialogues, interviews, lectures, and announcements. Listening strategies emphasized include summarizing main ideas, making inferences, and listening for stressed words, reductions, and intonation. A cassette tape program with instructor's key accompanies each text.

A Speaking Activities Book I, II: These books are designed to give students the opportunity to practice their speaking and listening skills in English by promoting realistic use of the language through individual, pair, and small-group work. Task-oriented and problem-solving activities simulate real-life situations and help develop fluency.

Instructor's Manual I, II: These manuals provide instructions and guidelines for use of the books separately or in any combination to form a program. For each of the core books except *Speaking Activities,* there is a separate section with teaching tips, additional activities, and other suggestions. The Instructor's Manual also includes sample tests for the grammars and readers.

The grammatical focus for the twelve chapters of *Interactions I* is as follows:

1. the simple present tense; pronouns
2. the present continuous tense vs. the simple present; *there* vs. *it;* the modals *can, may, might, will*
3. nouns; comparison of adjectives and adverbs; the modals *can, could, will, would, may;* the future with *be going to*
4. review; phrasal verbs
5. the simple past tense; *used to*
6. the past continuous tense; infinitives
7. more on infinitives; *should, had better,* and *must;* the reflexive; adjective clauses with *who* and *that*
8. review
9. the present perfect with *since, for;* the present perfect continuous
10. gerunds
11. the present perfect tense with *just, already, yet, still,* and so forth; the superlative
12. review

INTERACTIONS I: A WRITING PROCESS BOOK

Rationale

INTERACTIONS I: A WRITING PROCESS BOOK was designed to lead students through the writing process and provide a variety of activities to help them master the wide array of writing skills necessary for good writing. The text incorporates a number of features that set it apart from other writing books for nonnative students of English.

While most writing texts concentrate on the end product, INTERACTIONS I: A WRITING PROCESS BOOK shows students strategies that they can use in each step of the writing process.

The text consists of twelve chapters; each can be used for approximately four to six hours of classroom work. Each chapter is divided into twelve sections focusing on different steps in the writing process. These sections introduce various writing strategies and techniques and allow the students to practice them one step at a time. This practice helps the students understand how the different techniques work before they use them in their own writing. Students are given specific guidance in using their new skills to generate and organize ideas and to write, edit, and revise paragraphs of their own. At every step the students are encouraged to analyze and discuss the strategies they are employing. In this way, students focus on one skill at a time. Beginning students especially benefit from this step-by-step approach because they are usually more comfortable with structured practice. By the end of each chapter, the students have acquired new skills and have produced their own paragraphs.

In addition to the twelve chapters, there are appendices at the end of the book to provide spelling, punctuation, and capitalization rules that students can use for reference. There are also feedback sheets for the instructor's use (see Teaching Suggestions).

Although the concept of writing as a process is central to the course, traditional areas of instruction such as paragraph form, mechanics, and grammar are practiced throughout. The emphasis, however, is on grammatical and lexical features that serve to unify a paragraph.

Our own classroom experience shows that the analysis of model paragraphs can be helpful and instructive. Therefore, the chapters also contain two or three tasks based on model paragraphs.

Chapter Organization

Exploring Ideas: The first problem that most students encounter is a difficulty in generating ideas. This section teaches strategies to help them with that task. Some of the methods presented are discussing and listing ideas, interviewing, and free writing. A vocabulary-building activity provides students with some of the vocabulary they may need in writing their own paragraphs and encourages them to use fellow students and their teachers as resources for additional vocabulary development.

Organizing Ideas: In this section students are taught organizational skills such as writing effective topic sentences, limiting the information in a paragraph, and organizing different types of paragraphs.

Developing Cohesion and Style: The focus of this section is on the grammatical and lexical features that serve to unify a paragraph. Students are taught the most natural use of structures and vocabulary in extended written discourse. Some sentence-level structures that often cause students problems, such as choice of tense, are also covered in this section.

Using Correct Form: Each chapter provides practice with the mechanics of writing such as paragraph form, spelling, punctuation, and capitalization.

Writing the First Draft: Because most students do not realize that good writing is usually the product of many revisions, they are explicitly told that the first paragraph they write is only a draft.

Editing Practice: One of the most important skills for students to master is the ability to edit their work. This section provides them with paragraphs that contain common errors of form, grammar, cohesion, and organization. By finding errors in compositions they haven't written, students learn to critically evaluate their work with less anxiety. A positive approach to this step is recommended. Students should not be expected to find all errors, and working in small groups can make this activity more fun.

Editing Your Writing: After students practice editing, they are asked to edit their own compositions. Teachers can ask students to focus on specific aspects of their writing to make this step less frustrating. It is also suggested that students work with partners to help each other with this important step.

Writing the Second Draft: Only after students have had a chance to revise and edit their compositions are they required to hand in neatly written papers for the teacher's evaluation.

Sharing: Too often, students' interest in their writing ends once they receive a grade. This section provides ideas on how students can communicate with each other through their writing. Suggestions include using the writing as the basis of debate or discussion, creating class books with student paragraphs, and displaying writing on bulletin boards.

Using Feedback: This section enables students to use their teacher's feedback to help them evaluate their progress and take responsibility for improving their writing. At the end of the text, feedback sheets are provided. Teachers who wish to focus their feedback on the particular features covered in each chapter will find that these sheets provide an easy method for doing so.

Developing Your Skills: This section provides additional reading and writing assignments to reinforce the chapter's teaching points and themes.

Developing Fluency: Unstructured journal writing assignments, both on and off the chapter topic, are featured here for extra writing practice.

Teaching Suggestions

The text has been designed for four hours of classwork per chapter, with homework assignments after each class. Some groups may require more classroom time. Although the text provides a set format, this should not be considered prescriptive. More sophisticated students who may have already developed their own writing strategies should not be forced to abandon them. In addition, we recommend that you ask the students to do as much extra free writing as possible; the instructor's manual contains additional suggestions for assigning unstructured writing work.

Many tasks in the text are described as pair or group work. Though teachers should consider themselves free to adapt the tasks according to the needs and abilities of their own students, we feel that group and pair work helps students to develop self-confidence. Since writing is such a daunting task for most students, working with others may help them to see that all students have many of the same difficulties.

The feedback sheets at the end of the book are provided to help teachers organize their comments in a way that students can easily interpret. Teachers are encouraged to give as much positive feedback as possible, to focus on content before grammar, and to concentrate on those skills that are presented in each particular chapter. This is especially vital for beginning students, whose mistakes are so numerous.

Changes to the Second Edition

The second edition of *Interactions II: A Writing Process Book* remains dedicated to providing students with a variety of activities that guide them through the process of writing. However, each chapter of the second edition includes many new features. These are:

- More sentence-level language exercises
- More writing assignments, both structured and free
- Expanded editing exercises
- Updated and expanded material on the chapter topic for students to discuss and write about
- Clearer visual presentation of material
- Many new photographs

Each chapter also includes two new sections, **Developing Your Skills** and **Developing Fluency**. **Developing Your Skills** gives students additional reading and writing assignments to reinforce the chapter's teaching points and themes. **Developing Fluency** provides students with unstructured journal writing assignments, both on and off the chapter topic.

Acknowledgments

We would like to thank the many people who made these books possible: Mary McVey Gill, our editor, whose ideas, encouragement, and patience were invaluable; Marie Deer, responsible for taking the books through production; Pat Campbell, the copyeditor who smoothed over our rough edges; and Axelle Fortier, the artist, for bringing some of the characters to life. We would also like to thank the many educators who made us aware of the process of writing and the importance of discoursal features—and, finally, our students, the catalysts for all our ideas.

Our thanks also to the following reviewers whose comments, both favorable and critical, were of great value in the development of this text: Janet Anderson, Iowa State University; Lida Baker, University of California, Los Angeles; Marilyn Bernstein, Santa Barbara Community College; Laurie Blass; Sharon Bode, University of Southern California; Phillip Borchers, Arkansas State University; Ellen Broselow, State University of New York, Stony Brook; Joy Durighello, City College of San Francisco; Charles Elerick,

University of Texas, El Paso; Jami Ferrer, University of California, Santa Barbara; Anne Hagiwara, Eastern Michigan University; Charles Haynes; Nancy Herzfeld-Pipkin, San Diego State University; Darcy Jack, Los Angeles Unified School District; Patricia Johnson, University of Wisconsin, Green Bay; Debbie Keller, ELS Language Center, Decatur, Georgia; Gail Kellersberger, University of Houston; Elaine Kirn, Santa Monica College; Constance Knop, University of Wisconsin, Madison; James Kohn, San Francisco State University; Lois Locci, De Anza College; Barbara Mallet, College of Mount St. Joseph; Debra Matthews, University of Akron; Beverly McChesney, Stanford University; Sandra McKay, San Francisco State University; Lisa Mets, Vincennes University; Eric Nelson, University of Minnesota, Minneapolis; Helen Polensek, Oregon State University; Virginia Samuda, University of Michigan; Rodney Sciborski, Rio Hondo College; Trish Shannon; Elizabeth Templin, University of Arizona; Ann Thompson, University of Arizona; Mary Thurber, Community College of San Francisco; Richard Van De Moortel; Stephanie Vandrick, University of San Francisco; Patty Werner, University of California, Santa Barbara; Carol Williams, University of California, Riverside; Jean Zukowski-Faust, University of Arizona.

Thanks also to the following reviewers of the first edition for their help on the second edition: Anne Bonemery, James Burke, John Kopec, Linda Levine, and Christine Salica.

M. K. S.
C. P.

To the Student

Writing is like carrying things up steps. If you try to jump to the top with everything . . .

. . . you will have trouble.

If you carry small armfuls up step by step . . .

. . . you will reach the top.

STEPS TO WRITING

1. Exploring Ideas
2. Organizing Ideas
3. Developing Cohesion and Style
4. Using Correct Form
5. Writing the First Draft
6. Editing Practice
7. Editing Your Writing
8. Writing the Second Draft
9. Sharing
10. Using Feedback
11. Developing Your Skills
12. Developing Fluency

TALKING ABOUT WRITING

Look at the steps to writing.

1. What do you do in each step?
2. Why is each step important?
3. Do you use these steps when you write in your language?
4. Which steps do you like? Why?
5. Which steps do you dislike? Why?

Discuss how you write in your native language with other students in the class. Answer these questions:

1. How many times do you write and rewrite a paper?
2. Do you make an outline?
3. How do you think of ideas?
4. Do you talk to other people about what you write?
5. Do you check your paper for correct grammar, spelling, and punctuation?
6. Do you write in English the same way you write in your language?

Look at this material from papers written by teachers and graduate students.

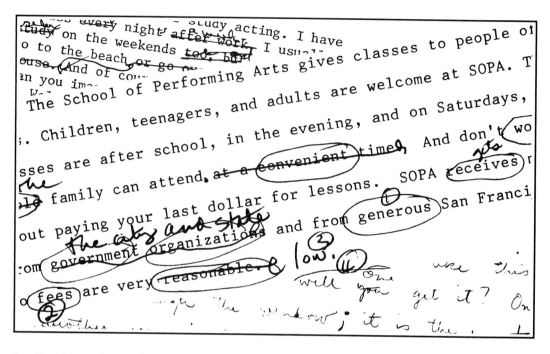

1. Do they write perfect papers the first time?
2. Do they change what they write?
3. Does your writing in your language look like these papers?
4. Now think about the pictures at the beginning of this preface. Why is writing like carrying things up steps?

M. K. S.
C. P.

INTERACTIONS I
A Writing Process Book

1

SCHOOL LIFE

GETTING READY TO WRITE

Exploring Ideas

Interviewing Someone

A. A reporter for a school newspaper is writing an article about the new foreign students on campus. She is interviewing some of the students. Look at some of her questions.

1. What is your name?
2. Where are you from?

3. What do you like to do in your free time?
4. What is your occupation?
5. What do you like about the United States (or Canada)?

B. You are going to interview one of the students in your class for an article for a book about your class. First write some questions. Use some of the questions above and write three other questions.

C. Your teacher will write some of the students' questions on the board. Discuss them. Are they good questions to ask? Now look at your questions. Are they good questions to ask?

D. Choose the ten questions you like most. Then choose a partner and interview him or her. Write your partner's answers after the questions.

Building Vocabulary

What new vocabulary did you or your partner use? Your teacher will list some of the new words on the board. Discuss the new vocabulary. Use this chart.

Work?	Free-Time Activities	Goals or Fields	Other New Vocabulary
waiter	swim	engineering medical technology	very much
_____	_____	_____	_____
_____	_____	_____	_____
_____	_____	_____	_____
_____	_____	_____	_____

Organizing Ideas

Ordering Information in a Paragraph

The reporter now renumbers her questions in the order she wants to write about. In this kind of paragraph, people usually write facts first and then opinions.

A. Look at the reporter's new set of questions.

1. What is your name?
2. Where are you from?
3. How old are you?
4. What is your occupation?
5. Why are you in the United States (Canada)?
6. What do you like about the United States (Canada)?
7. What do you dislike about the United States (Canada)?
8. How do you like this school?
9. What do you like to do in your free time?

B. The reporter interviews a student from Japan. Read her notes.

1. What is your name? _____ *Yoshi Hiramoto*
2. Where are you from? _____ *Chiba — near Tokyo — seaport*
3. How old are you? _____ *34 years old*
4. What is your occupation? _____ *sales manager*
5. Why are you in the United States? _____ *needs English for job*

6. What do you like about the United States? *likes class,
likes Americans*

7. What do you dislike about the United States? *doesn't like
cafeteria food*

8. How do you like this school? *very much, good English
class*

9. What do you like to do in your free time? *visits sights,
rides bicycle*

C. Renumber your questions in the order you want the information to appear in your paragraph. Then write the answers in the correct order. You don't need to write complete sentences.

D. Show your organization to your partner. Does he or she agree with it? Does he or she want to add any information?

Writing Topic Sentences

The topic sentence tells the main idea of the paragraph. You will learn more about topic sentences in other chapters of this book. In your paragraph, the topic sentence introduces your partner and tells something important about him or her. Don't begin paragraphs with "I am going to write about . . ." or "This paragraph is about . . ." You can begin your paragraph with "(Name of student) is a member of (name of class) at (name of school)." Write your topic sentence here:

_____

_____

PART TWO

DEVELOPING WRITING SKILLS

Developing Cohesion and Style

Connecting Ideas

Good writers connect the ideas in their paragraphs. A paragraph with connected ideas has *cohesion*. Good writers also use natural English phrases to make a paragraph easy to read. A paragraph with natural English has good *style*.

In this section of the book you will learn how to write paragraphs with cohesion and good style.

1. You will practice verb tenses. A cohesive paragraph has correct verb tenses.
2. You will learn about words such as pronouns that refer to other words in a paragraph.
3. You will learn grammar and vocabulary that improve the style of a **paragraph**.
4. You will learn special words that connect ideas. In this chapter, you will learn to use *and, but, so,* and *also.*

Look at the reporter's paragraph and circle the words *and, but, so,* and *also.*

International Student at Eastern Community College

Yoshi Hiramoto is one of 350 International students at Eastern Community College. He is from Chiba, a seaport near Tokyo. Mr. Hiramoto is 34 years old and is a sales manager for a hospital equipment company. His company sells equipment to American hospitals, so he needs English for his work. Mr. Hiramoto likes the United States very much. He also likes the students at his school. He thinks his English class is excellent, but he thinks the food in the cafeteria is terrible. In his free time Mr. Hiramoto likes to bicycle and visit tourist sights near the school.

Using *and* to Connect Phrases

When you want to say two things about a subject, use the word *and* to connect the verb phrases.

Example: Mr. Hiramoto is 34 years old *and* is a sales manager for a hospital equipment company.

Write sentences from the following phrases. Connect the phrases with *and*.

Example: Ming Su   is 26 years old
                    is from Taiwan

Ming Su is 26 years old and is from Taiwan.

1.   Amelia   swims
                plays tennis

_____

_____

2.   Jorge   is Venezuelan
              comes from Maracaibo

_____

_____

3.   Reiko   is 19 years old
              likes music a lot

_____

_____

4.   Salma   is married
              has two children

_____

_____

5.   Enrique   likes soccer
                plays every Saturday

_____

_____

Using *also* to Add Information

When two sentences give similar ideas, you can use the word *also* in the second sentence. Find the *also* in the reporter's paragraph about Yoshi Hiramoto. *Also* usually goes before the main verb in the sentence, but it goes after the verb *be:*

Examples: Mr. Hiramoto likes the United States very much. He *also likes* the students in his school.
            Janet is in my English class. She *is also* in a music class.

We use the caret symbol (∧) in corrections to add something to a sentence.

also

Example: She is very pretty.   She is ∧ very intelligent.

A. Use a ∧ to add *also* to these sentences.

1. He likes baseball. He likes rock music.

2. Hamid is tall. He is very athletic.

3. In her free time, Maddie plays basketball. She likes to swim.

4. Efraim works part-time. He takes care of his four children.

B. Look at your notes from the interview. Write sentences that connect similar information with *and* and *also*. Show your sentences to your partner. Are they correct?

Using *and, but,* and *so* to Connect Sentences

You can connect two sentences with *and, but,* or *so.* Use a comma before these words when they connect two complete sentences.

And introduces additional information.

Example: Students at some schools can study everything from Asian studies to zoology. +
There are many recreational facilities and student services. =
Students at some schools can study everything from Asian studies to zoology, *and* there are many recreational facilities and student services.

But introduces contrasting information.

Example: He thinks his English class is excellent. +
He thinks the food in the cafeteria is terrible. =
He thinks his English class is excellent, *but* he thinks the food in the cafeteria is terrible.

So introduces a result.

Example: His company sells equipment to American hospitals. +
He needs English for his work. =
His company sells equipment to American hospitals, *so* he needs English for work.

A. Connect the sentences with *and* or *but.*

1. Alberto lives with his sister. She drives him to school every afternoon.

_____

_____

2. Maria can speak English well. She needs more writing practice.

   _____

   _____

3. Western Adult School is in a beautiful location. It doesn't have very good library facilities.

   _____

   _____

4. The school offers a good program in business. Its recreational facilities are excellent.

   _____

   _____

B. Connect the sentences with *so* or *but*.

1. She has to work all day. She doesn't have time to do all her homework.

   _____

   _____

2. He likes his English class. He doesn't think the American students are very friendly.

   _____

   _____

3. Her company is opening an office in the United States. It needs English-speaking workers.

   _____

   _____

4. She likes school life. She is homesick for her family.

   _____

   _____

C. Look at your notes from the interview and write two or three sentences using *and, but,* and *so* to connect ideas.

_____

_____

_____

_____

_____

_____

_____

_____

Using Correct Form

Following Correct Paragraph Format

A. Look at the first draft of the reporter's paragraph, which follows. She didn't use good form. Read the rules that follow the first draft. Then find the reporter's mistakes.

international student at eastern community college
Yoshi Hiramoto is one of 350 international students at
eastern community college. He is from Chiba, a seaport near Tokyo
. Mr. Hiramoto is 34 years old and is a sales manag
er for a hospital equipment company . his Company sells
equipment to American hospitals, so he needs English for his
work.
Mr. Hiramoto likes the United States very much he also likes
the students at his school.he thinks his English class is
excellent, but he thinks the food in the cafeteria is
terrible. in his free time Mr. Hiramoto likes to bicyc
le and visit tourist sights near the school.

RULES FOR THE FORM OF SENTENCES AND PARAGRAPHS

1. Write the title in the center of the first line.
2. Capitalize all important words in the title.
3. Don't capitalize small words like *a, the, to, with,* and *at* in titles, except at the beginning of a title.
4. Skip a line between the title and the paragraph.
5. Indent (leave a space) at the beginning of every paragraph.
6. Begin every line except the first at the left margin. (Sometimes a line for the left margin is on the paper. If it isn't, leave a space of one inch.)
7. Leave a one-inch margin on the right.
8. Use a period (.) at the end of every sentence. (For rules on punctuation, see Appendix 3 at the end of this book.)
9. Leave a small space after the period.
10. Begin every sentence with a capital letter. (For rules on capitalization, see Appendix 2.)
11. Also capitalize names of people and places. (See Appendix 2.)
12. If the last word of a line doesn't fit, use a hyphen (-) to break it. You can break a word only between syllables (**e•quip•ment**).
13. Periods and commas (,) must follow words. They can't begin a new line.
14. Every sentence in the paragraph follows the sentence before it. Start on a new line only when you begin a new paragraph.
15. In formal writing, most paragraphs have four to ten sentences. A paragraph usually has more than one or two sentences.

B. Compare the first draft with the paragraph on page 6.

C. Rewrite the following paragraph. Use correct form. When you finish, check it with the rules on page 11.

Life at the university of California at berkeley
The University of California at Berkeley has an int
ernational atmosphere, so it is a good place for nonnative
speakers of English to study. it is in the beautiful hills
of a small city near San Francisco and has some of the best
facilities and most famous professors in the United States.
students at Berkeley can study eve
rything from Asian studies to zoology, and there are many
recreational facilities and student services. there is a
main library and nine small libraries these libraries have
over 5.6 million books life at this California school is
usually very informal

    students live in college dormitories and in apartments in
the city of Berkeley, and there are many interesting
activities and events in both Berkeley and San Francisco.

PART THREE

WRITING AND EDITING

Writing the First Draft

Write a paragraph about the person you interviewed. Use the topic sentence and the organization from Part Two of this chapter. You can also use some of your sentences with *and, so, but,* and *also.* You don't have to write everything correctly. You can check it and rewrite it later.

Editing Practice

Edit this paragraph and rewrite it correctly. Edit it two times. The first time, correct the *organization* of the paragraph (for example, Does it have a good topic sentence? Are all the sentences about one subject? Is the order of the sentences correct?) The second time, correct mistakes in capitalization and punctuation. Make any other changes you think are necessary.

A new class member

This is about Ana Maria vargas. is a new member of the English composition class at columbia Community College. There are many classes at columbia . she generally likes her life in the United States, but she doesn't like her apartment. She is 28 years old. Ana Maria is from Peru. She is married and she has three beautiful children. her children are young. so she doesn't work right now. In her free time Ana maria sings and writes songs.

Editing Your Writing

A. Look at the first draft of your paragraph. There are many ways to make corrections. Check your paragraph for:

1. Content

   Is the paragraph interesting?

2. Organization

   a. Are all the sentences about one person?
   b. Is the order of the sentences correct?
   c. Does the paragraph have a good topic sentence?

3. Cohesion and style

   a. Can you connect any sentences with *and, but,* or *so?*
   b. Can you add *also* to any sentences?

B. Check the paragraph for content. Is the information in your paragraph true? Is it interesting? Show it to your partner, the person you interviewed. Does he or she want you to add any information? He or she can help you edit your paragraph.

Writing the Second Draft

A. After you edit your paragraph the first time, rewrite it neatly. Use good handwriting and correct form. Then check it for:

1. Grammar[†]

   a. Are the verbs correct? Remember that third-person singular verbs end with *-s* in the present tense.
   b. Are the pronouns *he* and *she* correct?

2. Form

   a. Does the paragraph have correct form (indentation, capitalization, punctuation, and spelling)? Check the paragraph with the form of the paragraph on Yoshi Hiramoto at the beginning of Part Two.
   b. Is the spelling of all words correct?
   c. Is your handwriting neat?

B. Discuss your corrections with other students.

PART FOUR

COMMUNICATING THROUGH WRITING

Give your paper to your teacher for comments and corrections.

Sharing

Share your papers with your classmates. Read them aloud or pass them around the room.

Your class can also make a class book with your paragraphs. Students can type or write neat copies of the paragraphs with corrections and your teacher can make copies of them. You can give the book a title and share it with other English classes.

[†]Hint: Look for only one type of grammar problem at a time.

Using Feedback

When your teacher returns your paragraph with comments, look at it carefully. If you don't understand something, ask your teacher about it. The next time you write, look at your teacher's comments. Follow your teacher's instructions and try to correct any mistakes you find.

Developing Your Skills

As a class, interview your teacher. Write possible questions on the board. You can ask him or her:

1. Where are you from?
2. What do you like to do in your free time?
3. What do you like about your job?

Think of other questions, too.

Then write the paragraph together on the board. Remember the rules for organization, cohesion and style, grammar, and form.

Developing Fluency

You are going to keep a journal in this class. Journals are free writing exercises. A journal writing is called an *entry*. You can either buy a special notebook for your journal entries or write them on separate pieces of paper that you keep in a folder. Sometimes you will have a topic or a time limit to follow; sometimes you won't.

For your first journal entry, write for ten minutes about yourself. You can write about what you do, what you think of your school or your English class, or what you do in your free time. (Choose only one.) If you want, you can show your entry to your teacher or a classmate.

2

NATURE

GETTING READY TO WRITE

Exploring Ideas

Describing a Scene

Look at the picture. Then, in small groups, discuss these questions.

1. What is the title of the painting?
2. Who is Watson?
3. How is the weather?

16

John Singleton Copley, *Watson and the Shark*, 1778

4. How many people are there in this picture?
5. How do the men in the boat feel?
6. Is the man in the water afraid?
7. One man is holding something. What is he trying to do?
8. What can you see in the background?
9. Is this scene frightening?

Building Vocabulary

You are going to write a paragraph describing this scene. Here are some words you may need to write your paragraph. Find out the meaning of any words that you don't understand. Discuss the painting. Complete the chart with new words from your discussion.

Nouns	Adjectives	Verbs	Other
rowboat	huge	reach	_____
shark	frightening	kill	_____
spear	dark	hold	_____
rope	afraid	try	_____
oar	dramatic	attack	_____
background	_____	rescue	_____
ship	_____	_____	_____
teeth	_____	_____	_____
_____	_____	_____	_____
_____	_____	_____	_____
_____	_____	_____	_____
_____	_____	_____	_____

Organizing Ideas

Ordering Information in a Paragraph

Descriptions often begin with general information and progress to specific points. The first sentence gives a general description. This is the topic sentence.

A. Look at this paragraph. It describes the scene in the painting opposite.

> This is a picture of a park on a warm and sunny day. It seems very peaceful. In the park there are many large trees. On the left you can see a lake with some small sailboats. There are people in the park. They might be European. Some people are walking and some are lying or sitting on the grass. They are wearing old-fashioned clothes. The women are wearing long dresses and some of them are carrying umbrel-

las. In the middle of the painting there is a small child. She is walking with her mother. I don't like this painting very much because the people seem bored.

Georges Seurat, *Sunday Afternoon on the Island of La Grande Jatte,* 1884–1886

COURTESY ART INSTITUTE OF CHICAGO

B. Underline the topic sentence in the paragraph about the park.

C. Which one of the following sentences is a good topic sentence for a paragraph about *Watson and the Shark*? Circle the number.

1. *Watson and the Shark* is a good painting.
2. In this painting there are some men in a boat.
3. The men in this painting are afraid.
4. This is a painting of a dramatic rescue.

D. After the writer makes a general statement about the park, he or she gives details. Find the sentences that give details about the park. Then find the sentences that give details about the people.

E. At the end the writer gives an opinion. Find the sentence that tells you what the writer thinks about the painting.

F. Here are a student's notes about the picture that follows, *The Third of May, 1808* by the Spanish painter Francisco Goya. Arrange the notes in order from general to specific. Number them from 1 to 7 (1 is the most general). Put the writer's opinion last. Show your organization to another student. Does he or she agree with it? There may be several correct answers.

© ART RESOURCE

Francisco Goya, *The Third of May 1808*, 1814

a. _____   the men are kneeling

b. _____   some soldiers are getting ready to shoot some men

c. _____   this painting is frightening

d. _____   another man is praying

e. _____   it is nighttime

f. _____   this is a painting of an execution

g. _____   one man is holding up his arms

G. Make notes for your paragraph about the painting *Watson and the Shark* and organize them.

PART TWO

DEVELOPING WRITING SKILLS

Developing Cohesion and Style

Adding Details: Adjectives

Adjectives make descriptions more interesting. They can be in two different positions:

1. After the verbs *be, seem,* and *look.*

    Examples: The men are *young.*
                  The men look *horrified.*

    Note: If you want to use more than one adjective you can connect them with *and:*
    The shark is huge *and* frightening.

2. Before a noun.

    Example: The *young* men are in a boat.

A. Look at the picture *Watson and the Shark* again. With a partner, make a list of adjectives to describe:

-   the boat
-   the weather
-   the man in the water
-   the clothes the men are wearing
-   the shark
-   the water

B. Add the adjectives from your list to the following sentences.

1. The boat is in the water. _____

    _____

2. There is a shark in the water. _____

    _____

3. The men are wearing clothes. _____

    _____

4. The man in the water seems _____

    _____ .

5. The weather looks _____ and _____ .

Adding Details: Prepositional Phrases

A. Turn back to the paragraph about the Seurat painting of the park. Underline all the phrases that show position (of someone or something). Most phrases that show position begin with prepositions.

Notice that the prepositional phrases can be at the beginning of a sentence or at the end.

Examples: *In the park* there are many large trees.
There are people *in the park.*

It is good to put prepositional phrases in different places—not always at the beginning of a sentence, for instance. That way the style of your writing will be interesting.

B. The following sentences describe the painting *Peasant Wedding,* by Pieter Brueghel. Add one of the prepositional phrases from the list to each sentence. **More** than one answer is possible.

Pieter Brueghel, *Peasant Wedding,* 1568

in the center   on the floor
under the table   next to the table
to the right of center   at the table
on the left

1. There is a man who is pouring water _____.

2. There is a child _____ .

3. There are two men who are carrying food _____ .

4. There is a long table _____ .

5. There are two musicians _____ .

6. There are many people _____ .

7. There is a dog _____ .

C. Look at the notes you made about the painting *Watson and the Shark*. Use them to write sentences with prepositional phrases.

Using Articles: *a/an* and *the*

A/an and *the* are articles. They appear before nouns. *A* and *an* are indefinite articles. *The* is a definite article.

Examples: a bicycle   an umbrella   the record   the calendars

A/an and *the* have different uses. Usually *a/an* comes before a noun when the noun appears for the first time. After that, *the* appears before the noun.

Examples: This is *a* painting of *an* island near Paris. *The* island was a popular place to visit during the time of Seurat. *The* painting is very famous.

A. Complete the sentences with *a/an* or *the*.

1. There is _____ man on the left. _____ man is pouring water from _____ jug.

2. In the center there is _____ table. _____ table is very long.

3. Two men are carrying soup on _____ tray. Another man is serving _____ soup.

4. There is _____ child on the floor. _____ child is holding _____ bowl.

B. Look at your notes on *Watson and the Shark*. Underline your articles. Are they correct?

Using Pronouns

It is very important to use pronouns (words like *I, he, she, it*) when you write a paragraph. Pronouns help to connect your ideas.

A. Circle all the pronouns in the paragraph about the painting of the park. Then draw arrows to connect the pronouns to the nouns they represent.

B. The following paragraph, about the picture below (*Edo to Meiji*), seems strange because it doesn't have any pronouns. Change some of the nouns to pronouns. Then compare your new paragraph with a classmate's. Are the changes the same in both?

COURTESY TADANORI YOKOO

Tadanori Yokoo, *Edo to Meiji,* 1986

At the top of the picture is a woman. The woman is holding a fan. Beside the woman is a map of the world, and below the woman is a locomotive. Below the locomotive on the left is a man. The man is fishing. The man is sitting in a small boat. The painting is about Japan in the twentieth century. The painting shows how traditional Japan is blending, or combining, with modern Japan.

Using the Correct Form

Spelling Present Participles Correctly

The present continuous form of the verb has two parts, the verb *be* + the present participle (verb + *-ing*): for instance, *(I) am reading*. Here are some simple spelling rules for adding *-ing* to a verb.

SPELLING RULES FOR ADDING *-ING* TO A VERB

1. If the simple form of the verb ends in a silent *-e* after a consonant, drop the *-e* and add *-ing*.

    Examples: race/racing   move/moving

2. If the simple form ends in *-ie*, change the *-ie* to *y* and add *-ing*.

    Examples: die/dying   untie/untying

3. If the simple form is one syllable and ends in one consonant after one vowel, double the last consonant (except *x*) and add *-ing*.

    Examples: run/running   get/getting

    Note that *w* and *y* at the end of words are vowels, not consonants.

4. If the simple form ends in a stressed syllable, follow the rule above for one final consonant after one vowel.

    Example: begin/beginning

    If the last syllable is not stressed, just add *-ing*.

    Example: happen/happening

5. In all other cases, add *-ing* to the simple form.

A. Underline the verbs in the present continuous in the paragraph about the picture *Edo to Meiji.*

B. Write the present participles of the following verbs.

1. write _____
2. sing _____
3. drive _____
4. sit _____
5. stand _____

6. study _____
7. look _____
8. read _____
9. see _____

PART THREE

WRITING AND EDITING

Writing the First Draft

Write a paragraph about the painting *Watson and the Shark*. Use your notes. Remember to use the present continuous to tell what's happening. Use *there is* and *there are* to name the things in the painting. Don't worry about mistakes. You can correct them later.

Editing Practice

Edit this paragraph twice and rewrite it correctly. The first time, check the organization of the paragraph. Does it move from general to specific? Do you need to change the order of the sentences? The second time, check it for correct use of *a/an* and *the*. Make any other changes you think are necessary.

OIL ON CANVAS, 29 x 36 1/4". COLLECTION, THE MUSEUM OF MODERN ART, NEW YORK. ACQUIRED THROUGH THE LILLIE P. BLISS BEQUEST.

Vincent van Gogh, *The Starry Night*, 1889

The picture on page 26 is by a artist Vincent van Gogh. Our eyes follow the shapes up, around, down, and back again, like the ride on the roller coaster. It shows the starry night. In the front is a tree and in the center is an church, with other buildings around it. A moon and stars look like they are moving. I like this picture because it reminds me of the formation of the universe. It is the beautiful scene.

Editing Your Writing

A. Look at the first draft of your paragraph. Check it for:

 1. Content

    a. Are there interesting adjectives in the paragraph?
    b. Do the adjectives describe the picture well?

 2. Organization

    a. Does the paragraph move from general to specific?
    b. Do you need to change the order of the sentences?

 3. Cohesion and style

    a. Can you connect any sentences?
    b. Are the pronouns correct?
    c. Are the adjectives in the correct place?
    d. Are the prepositional phrases appropriate?

B. Ask your teacher for help if you need it. Then show your paragraph to a classmate. Does he or she want you to add or change anything? He or she can help you edit your paragraph.

Writing the Second Draft

A. Rewrite your paragraph neatly. Use good handwriting and correct form. Then check it for:

  1. Grammar[†]

     a. Are the verb forms correct? Is there an *s* on all third-person singular verbs? (The use of the *-s* ending on verbs is *subject-verb agreement*.)
     b. Is the use of *a/an* and *the* correct?

  2. Form

     a. Does the paragraph follow the rules for correct form? If you aren't sure, look back at the rules for the form of a paragraph on page 11.
     b. Are the present participles correct?

B. Discuss your corrections with other students.

PART FOUR

COMMUNICATING THROUGH WRITING

Give your paragraph to your teacher for comments and corrections.

Sharing

When your teacher returns your paragraph, share it with your classmates. Read it aloud or pass it around the room.

Using Feedback

Reread your paragraphs from this chapter and Chapter 1. Compare your teacher's comments. Do you see improvement in any area? Which area?

[†]Remember to look for these items one at a time.

Developing Your Skills

Find another picture and write a paragraph about it. After you edit your new paragraph, you can put the picture and paragraph on a bulletin board.

Developing Fluency

Write for ten minutes in your journal on anything you want.

3

LIVING TO EAT OR EATING TO LIVE?

GETTING READY TO WRITE

Exploring Ideas

Describing Holiday Foods

A. Discuss the picture. What are the people doing? What do you think they are eating?

B. You are going to write a paragraph about the special food you eat for a holiday. First, write in your journal about typical everyday meals in your country.

Write as much as possible in about five minutes. Don't worry about form or grammar.

C. Discuss your entry with other students. Make a list of the different kinds of food from the discussion. If you don't know the name of a food, describe it. Maybe your teacher or other students can help you.

Example: POPULAR FOODS

Name	Description
tacos	fried corn pancakes with meat and salad filling

D. Look at this list of dishes for the American holiday, Thanksgiving. Then think of the food you eat on a holiday in your culture. Make a list of the special dishes. Sometimes there is no English word for a special dish from your culture. Write the word in your language and explain it.[†]

Holiday: *Thanksgiving*   *stuffing*

turkey   *sweet potatoes*

cranberry sauce   *pumpkin pie*

Your Holiday: _____   _____

_____   _____

_____   _____

E. Write some sentences that compare the special food you eat on holidays with the food you eat every day.

Example: People usually prepare and eat more food on Thanksgiving. The Thanksgiving meal is more delicious than our everyday meals.

_____

_____

_____

_____

_____

_____

_____

Building Vocabulary

Look at these vocabulary words. Then in small groups, look at your classmates' sentences and make a list of words that are new to you. Are the new words nouns, verbs, or adjectives?

[†]Remember that some nouns are count nouns—you can count them—and some are not. In small groups, you may want to discuss which of the holiday foods on your list are count nouns and which are noncount nouns. Put a check (✔) after the noncount nouns. Some nouns such as *turkey* are sometimes countable and sometimes not. As a meat *turkey* is a noncount noun.

Example: How many *turkeys* are you going to buy? (count)
         Are you going to have *turkey* for Thanksgiving? (noncount)

Nouns	Verbs	Adjectives	Other
celebration	celebrate	joyous	_____
feast	_____	traditional	_____
dish	_____	typical	_____
_____	_____	_____	_____
_____	_____	_____	_____
_____	_____	_____	_____

© JERRY HOWARD/STOCK, BOSTON

Three generations at Thanksgiving dinner

Organizing Ideas

Ordering Information in a Paragraph

People often begin a paragraph with general ideas and then write more specific ones. The last sentence of a paragraph often describes a personal reaction, opinion, or feeling.

A. Look at the notes for the Thanksgiving paragraph.

1. Thanksgiving is a family celebration to remember the first harvest of American colonists

2. eat traditional foods from first Thanksgiving feast—many foods are Indian

3. eat turkey, stuffing, sweet potatoes, homemade bread, and pies

4. eat more food than usual, feel stuffed but happy

B. Make similar notes for your paragraph. Answer these questions in your notes.

1. What's the name of the holiday? What does it celebrate?
2. Why do people eat special dishes for this holiday?
3. What does your family eat on the holiday?
4. How do you feel about the holiday?

C. Organize these sentences into the correct order. Number them from 1, for the first in order, to 7, for the last.

1. _____   Everyone eats more than usual, and at the end of the day we are as stuffed (full) as the turkey.

2. _____   In my family, everyone brings a special dish for the Thanksgiving meal.

3. _____   My aunt bakes a turkey and fills it with stuffing, a mixture of bread and spices.

4. _____   Thanksgiving is a family celebration.

5. _____   They prepare many traditional foods such as turkey, sweet potatoes, and cranberry sauce.

6. _____   On this day Americans remember the first Thanksgiving feast of the early American colonists.

7. _____   My relatives also make bread, vegetables, salad, and at least four pies.

Writing Topic Sentences

The topic sentence:

- gives the main idea of the paragraph;
- is always a complete sentence and has a subject and a verb;
- is often the first sentence in a paragraph, but is sometimes the second or even the last sentence.

A. Which of these main ideas about Thanksgiving are complete sentences? Write a C in front of the complete sentences.

1. _____   The Thanksgiving meal is a special celebration.

2. _____   Thanksgiving, an important celebration.

3. _____   Families eat typical American dishes on Thanksgiving.

4. _____   A Thanksgiving feast for a family celebration.

5. _____   Thanksgiving is an important American holiday.

B. Look at the sentences about the Thanksgiving meal on page 34. Which sentence is the topic sentence?

C. Look at the notes you wrote for your paragraph. First, decide if you want to add or change anything. Then write a topic sentence for your paragraph. Remember, it may be the first or second sentence in your paragraph. Exchange your notes and your topic sentence with a partner and answer these questions:

1. Is the topic sentence a complete sentence?
2. Does it give the main idea that was in your partner's notes?

PART TWO

DEVELOPING WRITING SKILLS

Developing Cohesion and Style

Giving Examples with *such as*

When you write, you can introduce examples with the phrase *such as*. Connect the examples with the word *and*.

Example: On Thanksgiving Day we eat many traditional foods. The foods are turkey, sweet potatoes, and cranberries. →
On Thanksgiving Day we eat many traditional foods *such as turkey, sweet potatoes, and cranberries.*

A. Combine the sentences with the phrase *such as*:

1. On this holiday we eat a lot of fruit. The fruit includes oranges, pine-apple, and peaches. _____

   _____

2. On this day we like to eat many typical Mexican dishes. The dishes are tacos, meat or cheese enchiladas, and tamales. _____

   _____

   _____

3. We fill the dumplings with meats. We use pork, beef, and chicken. _____

   _____

   _____

B. Look at your list of special foods. Can you use *such as* to give examples of any of the foods? Write a sentence with *such as*. Then compare it to sentences by other students.

_____

_____

Using Appositives

When you talk about typical native dishes, you sometimes have to explain what they are. You can use an *appositive* to explain them. A comma goes before the explanation. If the explanation is not at the end of the sentence, another comma goes after it.

Examples: Turkey stuffing is a traditional Thanksgiving food. Stuffing is a mixture of bread and spices. →
Turkey *stuffing, a mixture of bread and spices,* is a traditional Thanksgiving food.

My mother fills the turkey with stuffing. Stuffing is a mixture of bread and spices. →
My mother fills the turkey with *stuffing, a mixture of bread and spices.*

A. Use appositives to combine these sentences.

1. A typical Middle Eastern dish is falafel. Falafel is a mixture of fried chick peas and spices. _____

_____

2. We eat dim sum. Dim sum is a kind of dumpling. _____

_____

3. People like to eat tempura. Tempura is fried shrimp and vegetables.

_____

_____

4. A favorite dish is chicken fesenjan. Chicken fesenjan is chicken in a spicy pomegranate sauce. _____

_____

B. Can you explain any of the typical dishes for your holiday using appositives? Write a sentence with an appositive. Then compare it to sentences by other students.

_____

_____

Using Correct Form

Using Commas with Appositives

Commas separate an appositive from the rest of a sentence.

Examples: On Easter, many people make Easter eggs, painted hard-boiled eggs.
My mother makes pfeffernuesse, a spicy German cookie, for Christmas.

Add commas to these sentences.

1. Rijsttafel an Indonesian rice and curry dish is popular in Amsterdam.
2. Americans often eat hot dogs pork or beef sausages on the Fourth of July.
3. For breakfast I like to eat blintzes pancakes with a cheese filling.
4. My friend makes great bouillabaisse a French fish soup.
5. Spaghetti an Italian noodle dish is popular in North America.

Forming Noun Plurals

Write the correct plural forms of these nouns. (See Appendix 1 at the back of this book for spelling rules.)

1. cookie _____
2. orange _____
3. peach _____
4. tomato _____
5. dish _____
6. pancake _____
7. cherry _____
8. knife _____
9. serving _____

Spelling Third-Person Singular Verbs

Write the correct third-person singular forms of these verbs. (See Appendix 1 for spelling rules.)

1. miss _____
2. watch _____
3. cook _____
4. eat _____
5. hurry _____
6. mix _____
7. play _____
8. wash _____
9. drink _____

PART THREE

WRITING AND EDITING

Writing the First Draft

Write your paragraph. Include the name of the holiday in your title, for example "A Thanksgiving Meal." Use the topic sentence and your notes from Part Two. Try to use *such as* and appositives in your paragraph. What tense will your sentences be in?

Editing Practice

Edit this paragraph twice and rewrite it correctly. First, find a place to add *such as* before examples. The second time check to see if the count and noncount nouns are correct. Make any other changes you think are necessary.

Special Christmas Foods

Christmas is an important holiday for many people in the United States. It is the celebration of the birth of Christ. People in North America prepare many special Christmas food from all over the world. Many Christmas specialties fruitcake and eggnog come from Great Britain. North Americans make fruitcakes with fruits, nuts, and liquors. Eggnog is a drink of eggs, milks, and sometimes rum. American also eat a lot of Christmas cookies. I love all the special Christmas food.

Editing Your Writing

A. Look at the first draft of your paragraph carefully. Check it for:

1. Content

    a. Is the paragraph interesting?
    b. Is the information clear?

2. Organization

    a. Does the topic sentence give the main idea of the paragraph? Is it a complete sentence?
    b. Are all the sentences about the holiday?
    c. Are the sentences in logical order?

3. Cohesion and Style

    a. Can you connect any sentences with *and, so,* or *but*?
    b. Are the appositives correct?
    c. Does *such as* introduce examples?

B. Look at your feedback sheets from Chapters 1 and 2. Is there anything you need to check carefully? Show your paper to another student. Does he or she understand your paragraph? Does he or she think you need to make any other corrections?

Writing the Second Draft

A. After you edit your paragraph the first time, rewrite it neatly. Use good handwriting and correct form. Then check it for:

1. Grammar

    a. Are the present-tense verbs correct?
    b. Are the count and noncount nouns correct?

2. Form

    a. Is the paragraph form (indentation, capitalization, and punctuation) correct?
    b. Is the spelling of words with *-s* endings correct?
    c. Is the use of commas with appositives correct?

B. Discuss your corrections with other students.

PART FOUR

COMMUNICATING THROUGH WRITING

Give your paragraph to your teacher for comments.

Sharing

Try to find pictures of the holiday celebration you describe in your paragraph. Bring family pictures or pictures from books to class. In small groups, read your paragraphs aloud and show each other the pictures you have.

Using Feedback

Look at your teacher's comments. If you don't understand something, ask about it. Then make a list of things you do well and the things you need to work on.

What I do well:

1. _____

    _____

2. _____

    _____

3. _____

    _____

What I need to work on:

1. _____

    _____

2. _____

    _____

3. _____

    _____

Developing Your Skills

A. Write about a typical evening meal in your country or culture. Describe the foods you eat. Then exchange your paper with a partner from another country. See if you have any of the same dishes.

B. Find a classmate from another country. Together, choose a special occasion you both celebrate, such as a wedding party or a birthday party. Then write about the foods you eat at this special occasion. After you write your paragraphs, exchange them. Are any of the foods the same?

Developing Fluency

A. Write in your journal for ten minutes about your favorite food.

B. Write in your journal for ten minutes about what you miss the most from your home country or culture.

4

GETTING AROUND THE COMMUNITY

GETTING READY TO WRITE

Exploring Ideas

Describing Places, Things to Do, and Directions

A good friend is coming to visit you. You are going to write him or her a letter. In this letter you will tell your friend about some of the things that you might do when he or she comes.

A. Complete this chart with places your friend might like to visit or things he or she might like to do. Write as many places and things as you can.

Places to visit:

1. _____
2. _____
3. _____

4. _____
5. _____
6. _____

Things to do:

	Inside		Outside
1.	_____	1.	_____
2.	_____	2.	_____
3.	_____	3.	_____

B. Compare your list with other students' lists. Are there any things you want to add or change?

In your letter you are also going to give your friend directions to your home. He or she is going to drive to your home.

C. Look at a map of your town or city. Will your friend have to take a highway? If so, how will he or she get from the highway to your home? Are there any important landmarks (such as a lake, tall building, park, etc.) to help him or her? Draw a map that shows the route from the highway to your home. Label all the important streets. Include any important landmarks.

Organizing Ideas

Organizing Paragraphs in a Letter

Your letter will have three paragraphs. Each paragraph has a different purpose. The first one will say hello, discuss the visit, and describe some of the activities you and your friend might do. The second paragraph will give directions to your home. The last paragraph will have only one or two sentences. The purpose of this paragraph is to say good-bye and end the letter.

Look at the following sentences. Decide if they belong in Paragraph 1, 2, or 3. Write 1, 2, or 3 on the line before each sentence. There may be more than one correct answer for each sentence.

a. _____   We can also go to a baseball game.

b. _____   There's a gas station on the corner.

c. _____   There's a concert at the City Auditorium.

d. _____   Make a left turn on Maple Avenue.

e. _____   Please write and tell me what time you will arrive.

f. _____   It won't be hard to find my house.

g. _____   It won't be easy to get theater tickets.

h. _____   I'm glad to hear that you are doing well.

i. _____   See you in two weeks.

PART TWO

DEVELOPING WRITING SKILLS

Developing Cohesion and Style

Using Correct Verb Forms

Complete the sentences with the correct forms of the verbs in parentheses. Use the simple form, the present or future tense, or *be going to*.

There _____are_____ (be) many things to do here. I'm sure that we _____will have_____ (have) a good time. It will probably _____is_____ (be) hot, so _____will bring_____ (bring) your bathing suit. There _____is going to_____ (be) a beach very near my home. I _____know_____ (know) you like music, and the London Symphony _____given_____ (give) a concert on Saturday night. On Sunday we can _____visit_____ (visit) the art museum or go hiking in Butler State Park.

Using Prepositions

Prepositions often show:

1. place

   Example: There's a store *on* { the right.
   the left.
   the corner.
   Main Street.

2. direction

   Example: Take Highway 6 *to* Exit 14.

3. distance

   Example: Go straight *for* two blocks.

A. Underline the prepositions of place, distance, and direction in the following paragraph. Then exchange papers with another student and compare them.

> Take Route 44 south to Exit 12. Turn right at the first light. You will be on Maple Avenue. Go straight down Maple Avenue for two miles. At the corner of Bryant and Maple you will see an elementary school. Turn right at the first street after the school. The name of the street is Roosevelt Drive. Go straight for five blocks. Then make a left turn onto Broadmoor. My apartment building isn't difficult to find. It's on the left, Number 122. You can park your car behind the building.

B. Complete the paragraph with the preposition below. There may be more than one possible answer.

at   on   in   to   for

Turn right _____ at _____ Smith Drugstore. You will be _____ to _____
                    1   2
Church Street. Go straight _____ to _____ Church _____ for _____ two
                                    3   4
blocks. Then turn left _____ at _____ the corner of Church and Findlay.
                              5
Go straight _____ to _____ one block. Then turn left _____ on _____
                    6   7
Hudson Drive. My house is the third one _____ in _____ the left.
                                                8

C. Look at the following map. Work with a partner. One student will write directions from the post office to the library. The other student will write directions from the supermarket to the park. Exchange papers. Can you understand your partner's directions? Make any corrections necessary.

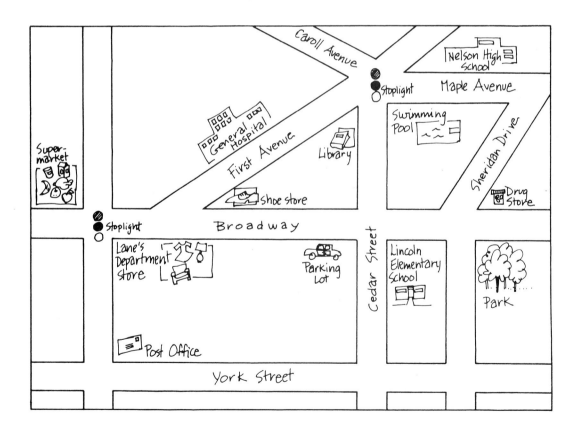

Using *there* and *it*

A. Look at these sentences.

> *There* is a supermarket on the corner.
> *It* has a big red and white sign.

The word *it* is a pronoun. It replaces a noun in a sentence. The word *there* does not replace a noun in a sentence. In the sentence above, what noun does *it* replace?

B. Complete the following paragraph with *there* or *it*.

_____ are many things to see in Washington. _____ is a
          1   2
very interesting city. In the center of the city _____ is a large
                                                                              3
open area. People call _____ the mall. All around the mall
                                              4
_____ are museums. In the center of the mall _____ is a
          5   6
very large structure. _____ is the Washington Monument.
                                        7

Using Correct Form

Writing an Informal Letter

This is a form of an informal letter.

DATE   July 12, 19XX

SALUTATION

Dear Bill,

I am excited about your visit. There's a lot to do here, and I'm sure we'll have a great time. On Saturday afternoon we can go to a basketball game. I think I can get tickets. In the evening we're going to go to Randy's house for dinner. After dinner we might go to a rock concert. I'm going to try to get tickets. If you want, on Sunday we can play tennis in the morning and visit the planetarium in the afternoon.

It's easy to find my house. Just take the Connecticut Turnpike east to Exit 5. Turn left at the first light. Then you will be on Bradford Boulevard. Go straight on Bradford for three miles. Then turn left on Apple. You will see a large supermarket on your left. Go to the second light. Make a right turn on Woodgate Road. My building is on the right, three houses from the corner. It's number 417.

See you in two weeks.

BODY

CLOSING

Sincerely,

Steve

DATE: The date usually appears at the upper right. The order of the date is month, day, year. Capitalize the name of the month and put a comma after the day and before the year. Do not use a comma in the year.

Example: April 4, 1999

SALUTATION: Most letters begin with *Dear.* Use the name that you usually call the person. In an informal letter a comma goes after the name.

Examples: Dear Professor Hudson,
Dear Dr. Fitzgerald,
Dear Mr. and Mrs. White,
Dear Melinda,

BODY: Indent each paragraph of the letter. In letters, paragraphs may have only one or two sentences. Although it is important to keep each paragraph on the same topic, the paragraphs in a letter do not always begin with a topic sentence.

CLOSING: The closing of a letter begins either at the left or in the center of the page. There are many different closings. The closing that you choose depends on your relationship with the person you are writing to.

Examples: Regards, }
Best, } for informal letters

Fondly, }
Love, } for letters to close friends or relatives

Addressing an Envelope

This is the correct way to address an envelope.

Carol Martin
128 Lake Drive, Apt. 8
Muskegon, Michigan 49441 } **RETURN ADDRESS**   **STAMP**
U.S.A.
ZIP CODE

ADDRESS { Mr. and Mrs. Daniel Kaufman
432 St. George St.
Toronto, Canada M56 2V8
POSTAL CODE

RETURN ADDRESS: Write your address in the top left-hand corner of the envelope.

ADDRESS: Write the address clearly. You may want to print it. Make sure the address is complete. If there is an apartment number, be sure to include it. It is also important to use the zip code or postal code.

PART THREE

WRITING AND EDITING

Writing the First Draft

Write your letter to your friend. Then address an envelope.

Editing Practice

Edit this letter and rewrite it correctly. First, make sure the form is correct (review the rules on pages 48 and 49). Then go through it another time and check the verb forms. Make any other changes you think are necessary.

June 15, 19XX

Dear Mary, I'm very glad that you visit me next week. We will to have a good time. It's easy to find my house. Make left turn at the corner of Broadway and Fifth Street. Drive down Fifth two blocks. Make a right turn on Henry Street. There are a park on the corner. My house is on the left side. It are number 150. the weather is warm so we might going hiking and swimming. Please to bring your photo album. I want see the pictures of your family.

Editing Your Writing

A. Edit the first draft of the letter you wrote. Check it for:

1. Content

    a. Are the activities interesting?
    b. Are the directions clear?

2. Organization

    Is each paragraph about a different topic?

3. Cohesion and style

    a. Are the prepositions correct?
    b. Is the use of *there* and *it* correct?

B. Exchange letters with another student and talk about them.

Writing the Second Draft

A. After you edit your letter the first time, rewrite it neatly. Use good handwriting and form. Then check it for:

1. Grammar

    a. Are the verb forms correct?
    b. Is there an *s* on third-person singular verbs in the present tense?

2. Form

    a. Is the date correct?
    b. Is the salutation correct?
    c. Do the paragraphs begin with an indentation?
    d. Is the closing in the right place?

B. Discuss your corrections with other students.

PART FOUR

COMMUNICATING THROUGH WRITING

Give your letter to your teacher for comments.

Sharing

Show your letter to another student. Can he or she understand your directions? He or she can try to draw a map from the highway to your house using your directions.

Using Feedback

Look at your teacher's comments. If you don't understand something, ask about it. Do you see improvement in any area of your writing?

Developing Your Skills

A. Write another letter to a friend. This friend is going to take a plane to visit you. Explain what airport he or she should fly into. Explain how to get from the airport to your house. (For example, should your friend take a taxi, a bus, an airport limousine? Should he or she rent a car?)

B. You want your friend to meet you for lunch at school. You are going to leave him or her a note. Explain in your note how to get from your house to school.

Developing Fluency

Write in your journal for ten minutes about a problem you had finding your way around a new place.

5

HOUSING AND THE FAMILY

GETTING READY TO WRITE

Exploring Ideas

Using a Lifeline

In this chapter you are going to write about a part of your life. You can make a lifeline to help you. This is a line that shows the important events of your life.

A. Draw a line down the middle of a piece of paper. The top of the line represents the year you were born, and the bottom of the line is the present time. You can write some ages along the line too, as in the example.

B. Relax and think about your life. Think in English, if possible, and also think in pictures. As you think, try to answer these questions:

1. What important things happened to me?
2. What important decisions did I make?
3. Who were the important people in my life?
4. How did I feel at different times in my life?
5. What were the important changes in my life?

C. After you think about your life, write some of the important events on the left of the lifeline and feelings about your life on the right. Write in English if possible, but don't worry about correctness or order. If you can't think of something in English, use your native language. You can use pictures and symbols, and you may also want to look at family photographs. Here is an example of Linda's lifeline and some photos from her life.

D. Show your lifeline to some other students and talk about your life. Ask each other questions. What do the other students think is interesting about your life?

Building Vocabulary

A. These new words are in the sample lifeline. Discuss their meanings and then add words that you and other students used.

Nouns	Verbs	Adjectives	Other
twin	was born	popular	_____
self-confidence	grew up	scared	_____
childhood	_____	shy	_____
_____	_____	_____	_____
_____	_____	_____	_____
_____	_____	_____	_____

B. Did you need to write any words or phrases in your native language? Look them up in a dictionary and write their meanings in English. Then write a sentence that uses each new word or phrase. Show your sentences to the other students in your group. Do they think you used the words correctly? Then your teacher will check your sentences.

Organizing Ideas

Limiting Information

You can't write about your whole life in one paragraph, so you need to choose one part of your life to write about. You may want to write about your childhood, your school years, or one important event in your life.

A. Look at the lifeline of the twin on the next page and discuss where a paragraph on a part of a life can begin and end.

B. Look at your own lifeline and decide what part of your life you want to write about. Draw lines to show where your paragraph can begin and end. Discuss your decision with other students. Answer these questions to help you decide what part of your life to write about.

Lifeline

Events

Was a twin in a large family

Went to school, different class from twin

- Not very much happened in childhood

- Became a teenager, swam a lot

When I was sixteen I taught swimming on weekends

- Graduated from secondary school

Feelings

< 0

- Always felt secure
- Always had a friend
- Was scared of strangers

< 5 – Separation was difficult but grew to like school

< 10 – Liked to read, swim

– Was shy, not popular
– Swimming gave me self-confidence

< 15   Enjoyed my job, became less shy

Came to States

< 20

1. Is the part you chose interesting? You may want to write about unusual or funny events in your life because they are more interesting.
2. Is the part you chose important? Because you can't write your whole life story in one paragraph, choose one important event or time.
3. Is the part you chose all about one topic? Don't choose many different events or times. Everything in your paragraph should be about one subject.

Making Paragraph Notes

Look at the part of the lifeline you chose and add information you think is important. Cross out information that is not about the topic of your paragraph.

Writing Topic Sentences

A. Look at these paragraph notes. For each paragraph, circle the number of the topic sentence that you think gives the main idea. Discuss your choices with your classmates.

Paragraph 1

-- was born a twin--very important to childhood
-- large family
-- always had a friend, felt secure
-- went to school and was in different classes from twin

Topic sentences:

1. Because I was born a twin, I had a very different childhood from most people.
2. Because I had a twin, I felt secure.
3. I didn't like school because I was in different classes from my twin.

Paragraph 2

-- teenage years difficult
-- liked to read, was shy, not popular
-- was a good swimmer
-- taught swimming on weekends
-- this gave me self-confidence

Topic sentences:

1. I wasn't popular as a teenager.
2. As a teenager, I taught swimming on weekends.
3. My teenage years were very difficult at first, but they ended happily.

B. Write a topic sentence that gives the main idea for your paragraph. Show the notes for your paragraph and your topic sentence to other students. Do they think you need to change anything?

_____

_____

Writing Titles

The title should give the main idea of a composition. It should also be interesting. It goes on the top line of the paper and is not a complete sentence.

A. Look at the possible titles for the paragraphs about the twin. Put a checkmark by the titles that you like. Why do you like them?

Paragraph 1	*Paragraph 2*
My Childhood	Growing Up
Born a Twin	Unhappy Teens
Difficult School Years	Teenage Years
My Childhood as a Twin	Teaching Swimming

B. Look at your paragraph notes and write a title for your paragraph.

_____

PART TWO

DEVELOPING WRITING SKILLS

Developing Cohesion and Style

Using the Past Tense

Because you are writing about events in the past, most of your sentences will be in the past tense.

A. Complete the following paragraph with the correct past-tense forms of the verbs in parentheses. For the spelling of verbs with *-ed,* see Appendix 1 at the back of this book.

Because I _____ (be) born a twin, I _____ (have) a
₁   ₂
very different childhood from most people. There _____ (be)
₃
always someone to play with and I always _____ (have) a friend.
₄
My mother said we _____ (feed) each other, _____ (play)
₅   ₆
together, and _____ (cry) when strangers came near. We
₇
_____ (do) everything together. When my sister
₈
_____ (need) special shoes, I _____ (want) them too.
₉   ₁₀
But life as a twin _____ (not be) always great. My mother
₁₁
_____ (be) always tired because she _____ (work) so hard.
₁₂   ₁₃
My father _____ (say) he _____ (hate) to come home
₁₄   ₁₅
because with my older brother there _____ (be) three screaming
₁₆
babies in the house. Even now I think that when I get something I want,
someone else will go without.

B. Look at your paragraph notes and write sentences with past-tense verbs about your life. Compare your verbs with those of other students. Can you use any of their words? Also be careful to use past-tense verbs only for completed events; don't write "I studied English for three years" if you are still studying English.

Combining Sentences with Time Words and *because*

When you write a paragraph that describes events, you can use time words to combine sentences. Some common time words are *before, after, when,* and *as soon as.*

Examples: *Before* I started school, I was very happy.

After I left high school, I got a job.

When my family said good-bye, I was very sad.

As soon as I came to the United States, I got sick.

You can also combine sentences with *because* to show reasons. To review how to combine sentences with *and, but,* or *so,* see Chapter 1.

A. Complete the following paragraph with *before, after, when, because, and, but,* or *so.*

I had a typical childhood, _____ my life changed _____
1   2
I was fourteen. We moved from our small village to Karachi, a big city in

Pakistan. _____ we moved, life in the country was wonderful for
3
me, but _____ I started school in Karachi, I became shy and
4
nervous. The other boys in my classes were tough, _____ they
5
laughed at my country ways. _____ I didn't like the other boys, I
6
became more interested in books. I always liked biology, _____ I
7
started to read about medicine. I was very unhappy at the time,

_____ I'm glad this happened _____ I finally decided to
8   9
become a doctor.

B. Finish these sentences. Use information about your life if you can.

1. When I became a teenager, I _____

_____ .

2. I came to this country because _____

_____ .

3. When I was a child, I _____

_____ .

4. After I left high school, I _____

_____ .

5. Before I started this class, _____

_____ .

6. I wasn't very happy, but _____

_____ .

C. Write at least two sentences about your life, using the information in your paragraph notes. Use *because, before, after, when,* or *as soon as.*

_____

_____

_____

_____

_____

Using Correct Form

Capitalizing Titles

In the title, capitalize the first word and all the important words. Do not capitalize the following kinds of words (unless they are the first word in the title):

1. conjunctions: *and, but, or, so*
2. articles: *the, a, an*
3. short prepositions: *at, by, for, in, of, on, out, to, up, with*

Write these titles with the correct capitalization.

1. an exciting life _____

2. all's well that ends well _____

3. a gift of hope _____

4. the best years of my life _____

5. going away _____

6. a happy ending _____

7. life in a new city _____

8. best friends _____

9. a new beginning _____

10. a wonderful experience _____

Punctuating Compound Sentences

When you use *and, but, so,* and *or* to combine sentences, a comma generally goes before the conjunction. Don't use a comma if the conjunction doesn't combine sentences.

Examples: My brother was ten at the time, and I was twelve.
            We went to school in the morning and played all afternoon.

Add commas to these sentences if the conjunction combines two complete sentences.

1. My parents didn't have very much money so we moved into my aunt's house.
2. I was happier and prouder than ever before.
3. We moved to Texas and lived with my brother's family.
4. I was happy to get the scholarship but I didn't want to leave my family.
5. My grandmother was the most important person in my life and I was very sad when she died.

Punctuating Sentences with Dependent Clauses

Clauses beginning with time words (like *when, before,* or *after*) or *because* are not complete sentences—they are dependent clauses. You must combine them with an independent clause—a clause that is a complete sentence by itself. If you don't combine them with an independent clause, they are sentence fragments. If the dependent clause appears at the beginning of a sentence, use a comma after it. If the dependent clause appears at the end of the sentence, don't use a comma in front of it.

Examples: When I was five, we moved to Caracas.
            We moved to Caracas when I was five.
            Because my father had a new job, we moved to Caracas.
            We moved to Caracas because my father had a new job.
            Sentence fragment: We moved to Caracas. Because my father had a new job.

A. Some of these sentences have correct punctuation and some don't. Write *correct* after the sentence if the punctuation is correct. Rewrite the sentence with correct punctuation if it is wrong.

1. *Before* we moved here we used to have many friends and relatives nearby. _____

    _____

    _____

2. *Because* my uncle was an engineer, he sent me to engineering school.

    _____

    _____

3. I left the farm, *as soon as* I could. _____

    _____

4. We moved to Colorado. *Because* the doctors said I needed a dry climate.

    _____

    _____

5. *When* I first came here, I loved the excitement of New York. _____

    _____

6. I came to the city, *when* I was five. _____

    _____

B. Look at the sentences you wrote in Exercise C on page 60. Check your punctuation.

PART THREE

WRITING AND EDITING

Writing the First Draft

Now write your paragraph about a part of your life. Use the topic sentence and the notes you made in Part Two. Combine some sentences with time words and *because, and, but,* and *so.* Remember to use the past tense when you write about completed actions.

Editing Practice

Edit this paragraph twice and rewrite it correctly. The first time, see where you can combine sentences with *and, but,* and *so.* (Remember to use correct punctuation.) The second time, correct past-tense verb forms. Make any other changes you think are necessary.

How I Became a Jazz Musician

I fall in love with jazz when I am five years old. I always heared jazz in the streets but for my fifth birthday my brother tooks me to a concert. There I saw a great saxophonist I decided to learn to play the saxophone. First I need a saxophone, I ask my father. My father say he no have money for a saxophone. I work for my brother, uncles, and cousins. I made a little money. then my father see I work hard. He gave me money for a saxophone. I listen to albums. My brother teach me. I practice every day. Soon I am a good saxophone player.

Editing Your Writing

A. Edit the paragraph you wrote. Check it for:

1. Content

   a. Is the information interesting?
   b. Is the information important?
   c. Is there an interesting title?

2. Organization

   a. Does the topic sentence give the main idea of the paragraph?
   b. Are all of the sentences about one topic?
   c. Should you change the order of any of the sentences?

3. Cohesion and Style

   Did you combine sentences with time words and *and, but, so,* and *because*?

B. Exchange paragraphs with another student and talk about your work.

Writing the Second Draft

A. After you edit your paragraph the first time, rewrite it neatly. Use good handwriting and correct form. Then check it for:

  1. Grammar

     a. Are your nouns, pronouns, and articles correct?
     b. Did you use good sentence structure (no sentence fragments)?
     c. Did you use the correct past-tense verbs?

  2. Form

     a. Did you use correct paragraph form?
     b. Did you capitalize the words in the title correctly?
     c. Did you use correct punctuation when you combined sentences?

B. Discuss your corrections with other students.

PART FOUR

COMMUNICATING THROUGH WRITING

Give your paragraph to your teacher for comments.

Sharing

If you want, let other students read your paragraph. You may want to show them pictures of you and your family, too. Discuss the experiences you wrote about. Did other students have similar experiences? Do you have questions about the other students' paragraphs?

Using Feedback

Look at your teacher's comments. If you don't understand something, ask about it. Then look at all the paragraphs you wrote before and the teacher's comments on them. Make a list of goals. Write down things you can do to improve your writing. Use these questions to help you write your goals.

  1. Are your paragraphs interesting?
  2. Are your ideas clear?
  3. Are you organizing your paragraphs well?
  4. Are you using good topic sentences?
  5. Are there any grammatical structures you need to practice?

6.   Do you need to use neater handwriting?
7.   Is your spelling correct?
8.   Are you using correct paragraph form?
9.   How are your punctuation and capitalization?
10.   Are you trying to write sentences that are too difficult?

Developing Your Skills

Write a paragraph or two about what you are going to do in the next five years. Share it with a partner if you wish.

Developing Fluency

A.   Write for ten minutes in your journal about the happiest time in your life.

B.   Write for ten minutes in your journal about the saddest time in your life.

6

EMERGENCIES AND STRANGE EXPERIENCES

PART ONE

GETTING READY TO WRITE

Exploring Ideas

Creating an Ending to a Story

A. Read this story.

> It was a day just like any other day. Marvin got up when his alarm clock rang at seven o'clock. He smiled as he put on his uniform. Then he stood up straight and looked at himself in the mirror. He saw a short, slightly overweight man with a small moustache and a kind face. "At least the uniform looks good," he thought. He liked the blue uniform. When he put it on, he felt important.

Marvin listened to the news while he made breakfast in his tiny kitchen. The announcer was saying something about a convict who had escaped from prison, but Marvin wasn't paying attention. He was thinking about his father. His father was disappointed with him. Marvin knew that. But it wasn't his fault that he was too short to be a police officer.

After he finished his breakfast, Marvin prepared to leave for work. He washed his breakfast dishes, watered his plants, and fed his cat, Amelia. He arrived at work exactly on time. He always did.

There was a lot of mail that day. Before he could make his deliveries, he had to sort the letters and packages. When he finished, he put the mail into his large brown bag, put the bag on his shoulder, and left the post office.

One of his first stops was Dr. Jordan's house. As he was putting the mail into the mailbox, he heard a noise inside the house. "That's strange," he thought. "The Jordans are on vacation. They won't be home until tomorrow." He decided to go and look in the window.

B. In this chapter you are going to write the ending to this story. Before you write you should think about Marvin. Look at these pictures. Which one do you think looks like Marvin?

1.    **2.**    **3.**

C. Think about Marvin's personality. Answer these questions and give reasons for your answers.

1. Is he lonely? _____

    _____

2. Is he confident? _____

    _____

3. Is he happy? _____

    _____

4. Is he neat? _____

    _____

5. Is he responsible? _____

    _____

6. Does he work hard? _____

    _____

7. What can you tell about Marvin from his apartment? _____

    _____

D. Think about an ending for the story. Use these questions as a guide.

1. What did Marvin see when he looked in the window?
2. What did he decide to do after he looked in the window?
3. Why did he decide to do this?
4. How did he feel?

E. Make notes for your ending, but do not write it yet.

Building Vocabulary

Ask the teacher to help you with any vocabulary words that you need. Add the new vocabulary to this list.

Nouns	Verbs	Adjectives and Adverbs	Other
murderer	hit	strong	_____
gun	shoot	frightened	_____
convict	arrest	_____	_____
safe	steal	_____	_____
_____	break in	_____	_____
_____	_____	_____	_____
_____	_____	_____	_____
_____	_____	_____	_____

You will have to write your ending in the past tense. Do you know the past forms of all the verbs you want to use?

Organizing Ideas

Using a Time Sequence

Writers use time words such as *before, after, as, when, while, then,* and *as soon as* to organize the information in a story. Look at the story about Marvin again. Make a list of the time words. Compare your list with another student's. Are there any words you missed?

Limiting Information

You must write your ending in one paragraph. The paragraph should have 100 to 150 words. It is important to limit what you want to say.

Look at your notes. Tell your story to another student. With that student discuss these questions.

1. Is my ending too complicated, or difficult for the reader to understand?
2. Did I include too much description?
3. Can I fit everything into one paragraph?

Writing a Title

A. The title of a story should be interesting and not too general, but it should not tell the reader how the story will end. Which of the following do you think is a good title? Circle the number. Why do you think it's good?

1. Marvin Runs Away
2. The Murder of Marvin
3. A Big Day for a Little Man
4. Marvin Catches a Thief
5. Marvin the Mailman

B. Give your story a title. You may use one of the above or make up your own.

PART TWO

DEVELOPING WRITING SKILLS

Developing Cohesion and Style

Using *when, while,* and *as* with the Past Continuous and the Simple Past Tenses

If you want to talk about two actions in the past and one action interrupts the other, use *when* to introduce the interrupting action.

Example: The robber was opening the safe *when* the police officer came in.

Use *while* or *as* to introduce the action in progress, the action that *was happening*.

Examples: *While* the robber was opening the safe, the police officer came in.
As the robber was opening the safe, the police officer came in.

Use *while* or *as* when the two actions happen at the same time.

Examples: One robber was opening the safe *while* the other one was watching for the police.
Marvin listened to the radio *as* he ate breakfast.

Use *when* if one action follows the other.

Example: *When* the police officer entered the house, he heard a noise.

A. Combine these sentences with *when, while,* or *as.* More than one answer may be correct.

1. Marvin was looking in the window. Someone grabbed his arm. _____

   _____

2. The man grabbed his arm. Marvin started to fight. _____

   _____

3. A neighbor saw the fight. He called the police. _____

   _____

4. One robber was in the house stealing the jewelry. Marvin and the

   other robber were fighting. _____

   _____

   _____

5. Dr. Jordan gave Marvin a reward. He heard the story. _____

   _____

B. Look at the notes for your story and write three sentences: one with *when,* one with

while, and one with *as.* _____

_____

_____

_____

_____

_____

_____

Using *as soon as*

As soon as is similar to *when.*

Examples: As soon as he saw the thief, he ran away.
               He ran away *as soon as* he saw the thief.

However, *as soon as* emphasizes that one action happened *immediately* after another.

A. Combine these sentences with *as soon as*. For each pair of sentences, decide if *as soon as* goes at the beginning or in the middle of the sentence.

1. The thief saw Marvin. He started to run. _____

    _____

2. Marvin called an ambulance. He saw Dr. Jordan. _____

    _____

3. The police arrived. They arrested Marvin. _____

    _____

4. The neighbor ran outside. He heard the shot. _____

    _____

B. Look at the notes for your story and write two sentences with *as soon as*.

Using *then*

You can use *then* when you are narrating a story. By using *then,* you can make the time sequence clear and not repeat the same words. Compare:

Examples: I ran out of the house. After I ran out of the house, I saw a man in the street.
I ran out of the house. *Then* I saw a man in the street.

Varying Time Words and Phrases

Now you have learned several different time words:

when   *while*   *as*   *before*   *after*   *then*   *as soon as*

Although these words do not have exactly the same meaning, you can use some of them in place of others.

Examples: *When* he saw the thief, he called the police.
He called the police *as soon as* he saw the thief.

After he saw the thief, he called the police.
He saw the thief. *Then* he called the police.
He saw the thief *before* he called the police.

To make your writing more interesting, it is important to vary the words you use. Complete the sentences with the time words listed above.

Marvin put down his mailbag. _____ he tiptoed over to the window.
$_1$
_____ he looked inside, he saw a man's shadow. _____ he
$_2$ $_3$
had to make a decision. Should he call the police or should he go into the

house? _____ he was thinking, Marvin heard two voices
  4

from inside the house. There were *two* men! _____
                                                            5

he realized this, he knew he couldn't go into the house

alone, and he decided to go call the police. _____
                                                            6

he could leave the window, he felt a hand on his arm.

Using Descriptive Words

An interesting story tells the reader more than just what happened. It also describes
important people or places. Underline the descriptive words and phrases in the story
about Marvin. Then look at the notes for your paragraph. Add adjectives that describe
the people and places.

Using Correct Form

Using Quotations

A good story also tells the reader what the characters are thinking.

A. In the story about Marvin, the writer used quotations to show what Marvin was
thinking. Underline the sentences that tell you about Marvin's thoughts. Then look
at the notes for your paragraph again. Write down some of Marvin's thoughts that
you will include.

When you write exactly what someone said or thought, you use quotation marks. Use
quotation marks in pairs. Use one set at the beginning of the quotation and one at the
end.

Examples: "He looks like a thief!" Marvin thought.
              Marvin thought, "He looks like a thief!"

A quotation is always set off from the rest of the sentence by a comma, a question
mark, or an exclamation point.

Examples: "I should call the police," Marvin thought.
              "Maybe," Marvin thought, "I should call the police."
              "Stop those men!" Marvin yelled.
              "Should I try to stop them?" Marvin asked himself.

B. Look at these sentences. Put quotation marks in the correct places.

  1. Marvin thought, Who are those men?

  2. You should be a policeman, Marvin's father said.

  3. Come out of there! Marvin yelled.

  4. Do you have a gun? Marvin asked.

C. Look at the quotations you wrote for your ending and add quotation marks.

PART THREE

WRITING AND EDITING

Writing the First Draft

Now write your ending to the story about Marvin. Remember to:

1. use time words where they are necessary;
2. include descriptive words;
3. use quotations.

Editing Practice

Edit this paragraph twice. The first time, check that all the information is really important. Are there any sentences you can take out? The second time, check that the writer has used time expressions correctly. Make any other changes you think are necessary.

Marvin saw a man, while he looked in the window. It was a small, rectangular window. As soon as he decided to go inside. He walk around to the back door. Before he opened the door. He looked in the back window. The back window was large. Then he thought maybe the man had a gun. Marvin decided to call the police. Suddenly, he heard a woman scream. "There's a man looking in the kitchen window!" Before Marvin heard the voice he knew the answer to the mystery. Dr. Jordan and his family were home.

Editing Your Writing

A. Edit the paragraph you wrote. Check it for:

1. Content

   a. Is the story clear?
   b. Is all the information important?

2. Organization

   a. Did you use time words where necessary?
   b. Did you add a title?

3. Cohesion and style

   a. Did you vary the time words and expressions?
   b. Did you include enough description?
   c. Did you use quotations?

B. Exchange paragraphs with another student and talk about your work.

Writing the Second Draft

A. After you edit your paragraph the first time, rewrite it neatly. Use good handwriting and correct form. Then check it for:

1. Grammar

   a. Did you use the correct forms of the past tense?
   b. Did you use the correct forms of the present continuous tense?
   c. Did you use good sentence structure (no fragments)?

2. Form

   a. Did you use commas correctly?
   b. Did you use quotation marks correctly?

B. Discuss your corrections with other students.

PART FOUR

COMMUNICATING THROUGH WRITING

Give your paragraph to your teacher for comments.

Sharing

Read your ending to the other students in the class.

Using Feedback

Look at your teacher's comments. If you don't understand something, ask about it. There are some common editing symbols that your teacher may use. In Chapter 1 you learned about the caret (∧).

Example: ∧*The* Thief ran out the door.

Here are some others:

sp = wrong spelling   *l* = take out this word, letter, or punctuation

sf = sentence fragment   *○* = add punctuation here

Rewrite these sentences.

1. The police oficer helped Marvin. _____

   _____

2. Then, he went to the police station. _____

   _____

3. When he arrived there. He saw Dr. Jordan. _____

   _____

4. While he was talking to the doctor, Marvin came in. _____

   _____

5. Marvin's father *was* proud of him. _____

   _____

Developing Your Skills

A. Write about the strangest experience you have ever had. Explain what happened and why you thought it was strange. Share your writing with a classmate.

B. Write about the most dangerous or frightening experience you have ever had. Explain what happened and what you did. Share your experience with a classmate.

Developing Fluency

Write in your journal for ten minutes about anything you wish.

7

HEALTH AND ILLNESS

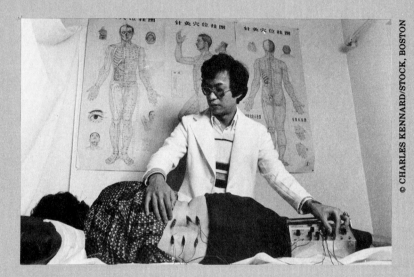

© CHARLES KENNARD/STOCK, BOSTON

GETTING READY TO WRITE

Exploring Ideas

Discussing Modern and Traditional Remedies

A. Look at these pictures and discuss them. What kinds of treatments are the people using? What do you think of these treatments?

B. Discuss these questions in small groups.

1. What do people in your culture do when they have colds? Do they usually take modern medicines? What traditional treatments do they use?

© PAOLO KOCH/PHOTO RESEARCHERS, INC.

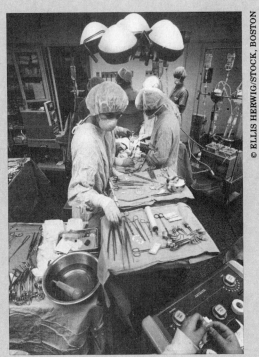

© ELLIS HERWIG/STOCK, BOSTON

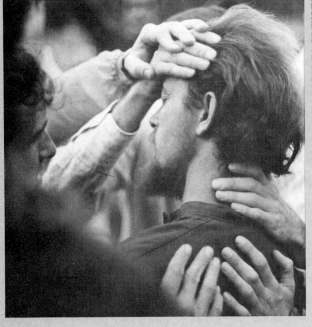

© ALAN CAREY/THE IMAGE WORKS

2. What do you do when you have a cold? Do you think modern treatments or traditional treatments are better?
3. What other traditional treatments do people in your culture use? What do you
   think of them? Do the people in your group know about any similar treatments?

Building Vocabulary

Add new words or expressions you used in your discussion to this list.

Nouns	Verbs	Adjectives	Other
treatment	treat	psychic	_____
acupuncture	heal	_____	_____
needles	take (medicine)	_____	_____
symptoms	massage	_____	_____
healer	relieve	_____	_____
_____	_____	_____	_____
_____	_____	_____	_____
_____	_____	_____	_____
_____	_____	_____	_____

Organizing Ideas

Making an Idea Map

You are going to write a paragraph about traditional treatments that people in your
culture sometimes use.

A. To get your ideas on paper, make an "idea map." Write the words *Traditional Treatments* in the middle of a piece of paper. Then write all your ideas about that topic
around the paper. Connect the ideas that go together. Look at the example of an
idea map of traditional treatments popular in the United States and Canada on the
next page.

B. Look at your idea map and make a list of the ideas you think would make a good
paragraph. Use these questions to help you decide.

1. Is the information interesting?
2. Do you have enough information for a paragraph?
3. Can you limit the information to a single paragraph?
4. How do you want to organize your information?

   a. the different ways people use one kind of treatment
   b. the different treatments people use for one illness
   c. a short description of several different treatments you are familiar with

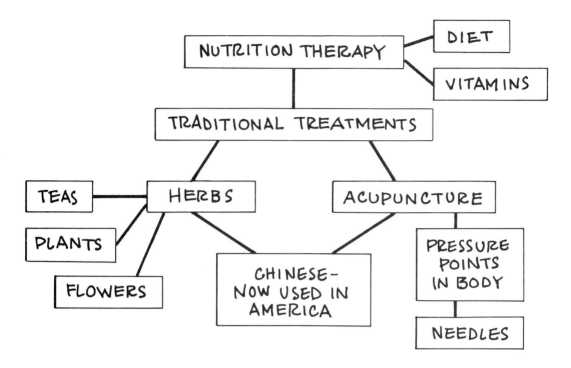

Writing Topic Sentences

A. Circle the letter of the best answer.

1. Choose the best topic sentence for a paragraph about herbs.
   a. People often make teas with herbs to cure sore throats.

   b. People in my country use herbs to treat many different diseases.

   c. I don't think herbs are as good as modern medicines.

2. Choose the best topic sentence for a paragraph about traditional treatments for colds.
   a. You don't have to spend a lot of money at a pharmacy to treat a cold.

   b. Lemon juice is a good traditional treatment for colds.

   c. I had a horrible cold a year ago.

3. Choose the best topic sentence for a paragraph about several different traditional treatments popular in the United States and Canada.

   a. One traditional treatment people in the United States and Canada often use is massage.

   b. People in the United States and Canada often go to nutritionists.

   c. Many people in the United States and Canada are using traditional treatments instead of modern medicine to treat a variety of health problems.

B. Write a topic sentence for your paragraph.

_____

_____

PART TWO

DEVELOPING WRITING SKILLS

Developing Cohesion and Style

Unifying a Paragraph with Synonyms

Writers often use synonyms (words with the same or a similar meaning) in their paragraphs. Synonyms unify a paragraph. When writers use synonyms, they don't have to repeat the same word many times.

Writers have to be careful when they use synonyms because very few words have exactly the same meaning. Look at these synonyms you might want to use in your paragraph. Read the definitions. Then complete the sentences that follow with the correct form of an appropriate synonym. There may be more than one correct answer for some of the sentences.

Nouns

treatment = anything people use to try to cure a disease or improve health
cure = a medicine or treatment to make a disease go away
remedy = a medicine or treatment that relieves symptoms
medicine (usually noncount) = (1) the science of health; (2) a drug a person takes to get over a sickness

1. When I have a cold, I take _____ three times a day.

2. I had several acupuncture _____ , but I did not get better.

3. Scientists don't have any _____ for cancer.

4. The best _____ for a cold is rest, even though doctors

   have no single cure.

Nouns

sickness = a health problem
illness = sickness
disease = a kind of sickness, usually serious
health problem = general trouble with health

5. Malaria and tuberculosis are dangerous _____ .

6. The cold is a very common _____ .

7. Although the doctor couldn't find any one _____ , my

   aunt still has _____ .

Verbs

to treat = to try to make a health condition better
to cure = to make a disease go away
to heal = to become whole; to improve a health condition like a broken bone or a
   scratch

8. The doctor is _____ her poor health with massage, good

   nutrition, and herbs, but she still doesn't feel very good.

9. A psychic _____ my cousin's asthma. He is completely

   well now.

10. My friend's broken arm is _____ very nicely now.

Using Restrictive Relative Clauses

Good writers combine short sentences with relative pronouns to make longer, more natural sentences.

Example: There are many people in the United States and Canada.
   They are trying acupuncture. →
   There are many people in the United States and Canada *who* are trying
   acupuncture.

Notice that *who* replaces the subject of the second sentence.

A. Combine these sentences with the relative pronoun *who* or *that*. Use *who* for people and *that* for people or things.

1. Acupuncture is an ancient form of medicine. Acupuncture developed in China. _____

    _____

2. An acupuncturist is a person. This person uses needles to treat diseases. _____

    _____

3. Many people find acupuncture helpful. They experience pain.

    _____

    _____

4. The acupuncturist puts a needle into the patient's body. The needle stimulates a special point. _____

    _____

    _____

5. Acupuncturists also use herbs. These herbs help treat the problem.

    _____

    _____

6. Some acupuncturists practice in the United States and Canada. These acupuncturists studied in China. _____

    _____

B. Complete these sentences with relative clauses that begin with *who* or *that*.

1. There are many traditional remedies _____

    _____ .

2. People _____

    often use herbs to treat diseases.

3. One remedy _____

    isn't very common in modern times.

4. I knew a woman _____ .

5. There are many plants _____

    _____ .

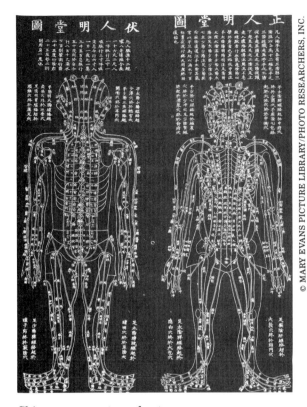

© MARY EVANS PICTURE LIBRARY/PHOTO RESEARCHERS, INC.

© PETER MENZEL/STOCK, BOSTON

Chinese acupuncture chart   Herbal remedies, Peru

Using Transitional Words and Phrases: *in addition, for example,* and *however*

Transitional words and phrases help unify a paragraph. They explain the connection between two or more thoughts. They often come at the beginning of a sentence.

Adding Information: *in addition*

In addition is similar to *and* and *also.* Use *in addition* when you are adding information after a long sentence or after several sentences.

Example: People used to drink special teas to cure many illnesses. Herbalists made some of these teas from the bark of certain trees. *In addition,* they sometimes made a cream with certain kinds of bark to put on cuts and bruises.

Giving Examples: *for example*

Use *for example* when you want to give specific examples.

Example: Many people go to psychic healers. *For example,* my cousin went to a psychic healer who cured his high fever with the touch of her hands.

Giving Contrasting Information: *however*

However is similar to *but*, but it often appears in more formal writing.

Example: Some psychic healers can cure many diseases. *However,* others just take people's money and don't help them.

Complete the sentences with *in addition, for example,* or *however.*

1. There are many Chinese acupuncturists in Canada. Many of them studied acupuncture in China and then immigrated to Canada. _In addition_, many Canadian doctors are now giving acupuncture treatments.

2. I often drink herbal teas when I am sick. _however_, if I am very sick I take modern medicine.

3. Some people in California use many traditional treatments. _For example_, they use Indian remedies and treatments that immigrants brought from their countries.

4. My grandmother often goes to an old lady who gives her strange treatments. _However_, these treatments don't usually help her.

5. I take lemon juice for colds. I put it in a cup of warm water and drink it several times a day. _In addition_, I take it for sore throats and fevers.

Giving Reasons and Examples

Read this paragraph and answer the questions that follow.

You don't have to spend a lot of money at a pharmacy to treat a cold. There are many old remedies that are just as good as the newer ones. For example, my grandmother always advised us to drink honey and lemon juice in hot water when we had coughs. People who study natural medicine now say that lemon juice is good for colds because it kills germs. I'm not sure why honey is good for colds, but I always feel better after I take it. In addition, my mother used to put me in a room full of steam to help me breathe better when I had a cold. Because scientists don't know how to kill viruses, there aren't any cures for colds, which viruses cause. I think honey, lemon juice, and steam are safer than chemicals with long names I can't pronounce.

1. Does the underlined sentence give a reason or an example? _____ ~~reason~~ Example

2. What expression introduces the first example of a traditional treatment? _____ is _____ advise us to drink honey and lemon in hot water

3. What was the second example of a traditional treatment? What words showed that it was additional information? _____ put in a room full of steam cough

4. *Because* introduces clauses of reason or purpose. An infinitive (*to* + verb) can also show purpose. Find an example of an infinitive expression that shows purpose.

_____

_____

Using Correct Form

Using Commas with Transitional Words and Phrases

Transitional words often begin sentences. A comma usually comes after a transitional word.

Example: In addition, people use hot peppers to treat colds.

A. After each sentence write another sentence that begins with *for example, in addition,* or *however.* Put commas after the transitional words.

1. I don't use traditional treatments. _____

_____

2. Many herbal teas are good for digestion. _____

_____

3. She went to a nutritionist. _____

_____

4. Psychologists can help you with many problems. _____

_____

5. It's important to have healthful foods. _____

_____

B. Add commas to this paragraph. Remember to use commas after transitional words and after dependent clauses that begin sentences. Use commas before conjunctions when you combine two complete sentences.

Some people can cure themselves of cancer with traditional treatments. For example I know a woman who cured herself of cancer by fasting. She didn't eat for one month and then she slowly began to eat again. When she completed the fast she had completely cured herself of cancer. In addition I read about a man who cured his cancer using an old Chinese diet. As soon as he started the diet he began to get better.

WRITING AND EDITING

Writing the First Draft

Now write your paragraph about traditional treatments that people in your culture use. Give reasons and examples when you can. Use these expressions:

1. examples: *for example*
2. reasons: *because, to* + verb
3. additional reasons or examples: *in addition, also*

Give your opinion in the last sentence of your paragraph.

Editing Practice

Edit this paragraph twice and rewrite it correctly. The first time, check for the use of transitional words and phrases. Do you need to add any? (Don't forget to use the correct punctuation for transitional expressions.) The second time, correct noun and verb forms. Make any other changes you think are necessary.

Jethro Kloss was an herbalist. He treated many Americans that doctors couldn't help. He write a book that was very important in the movement back to traditional treatments. Mr. Kloss encouraged the use of natural remedy. Example, he said that a good diet with plenty of fruit and vegetables was very

Chinese herbal medicines

important. As a treatment for disease, he recommend special cold and hot water baths. He advised his patients to get a lot of exercise. He recommended massage. Because he knew about hundreds of herbs, he was one of the most famous herbalists in the United States.

Editing Your Writing

Now edit the paragraph you wrote. Check it for:

1. Content

    a. Is the information interesting?
    b. Are there reasons and examples in the paragraph?

2. Organization

    a. Does the topic sentence give the main idea of the paragraph?
    b. Are all the sentences about the topic of the paragraph?

3. Cohesion and style

    a. Did you use synonyms correctly?
    b. Did you use relative clauses correctly?
    c. Did you use transitional words and phrases correctly?

Writing the Second Draft

A. After you edit your paragraph the first time, rewrite it neatly. Use good handwriting and correct form. Then check it for:

   1. Grammar

      a. Did you use correct noun forms?
      b. Did you use correct verb forms?

   2. Form
     Are there commas after transitional words and after dependent clauses?

B. Discuss the corrections you made with other students.

PART FOUR

COMMUNICATING THROUGH WRITING

Give your paragraph to your teacher for comments.

Sharing

The class can make a short book of traditional treatments throughout the world. Type or write your paragraphs neatly and make a book with them. Maybe someone in the class can draw some pictures for the book. You can give your book to another English class to read.

Using Feedback

Look at your teacher's comments. If you don't understand something, ask about it.

A. Read these symbols that many people use to correct writing.

   sp The spelling is wrong.

   vt The tense of the verb is wrong.

   ro You wrote a *run-on* sentence. A run-on sentence is an incorrect sentence that should be two sentences:

                                              ro

     He ate only junk food and never exercised, in addition he stayed up late nearly every night.

↻↘ You should move the circled part to where the arrow points.

≡ Capitalize the letter.

ww The word is wrong. Some words are almost synonyms, but each has special
uses.

                 ww
I like to swim to rest.

B. Rewrite these sentences correctly.

1. many people in the Philippines drink herb teas. _____

_____

2. The healer gave (to my friend) a foot massage.↘_____

_____

3. Three years ago he *wt* have a stomach ache. _____

_____

4. His leg did not *ww* cure. _____

_____

5. My friend didn't like to go to doctors, *ro* he went to a psychic. _____

_____

Developing Your Skills

A. Find a classmate who has an unusual or different remedy for a common problem
such as a cold, a headache, a sore throat, or a cough. Write about your classmate's
remedy.

B. Have you ever tried a new or unusual remedy? Did it work? Write about it and tell
whether it worked.

Developing Fluency

A. Write in your journal for fifteen minutes about the things you do to stay healthy.

B. Write in your journal for fifteen minutes about something you do that isn't very
good for your health.

8

TELEVISION AND
THE MEDIA

GETTING READY TO WRITE

Exploring Ideas

Describing and Categorizing Movies

A. Look at the photos from these movies and match them with the movie categories
below:

musical	comedy	horror
science fiction	detective	adventure

1. *The African Queen*

   Category: _____

2. *A Night at the Opera*

   Category: _____

3. Nosferatu

   Category: _____

4. *Singing in the Rain*

   Category: _____

5. *The Maltese Falcon*

   Category: _____

6. *Godzilla*

   Category: _____

B. Discuss these questions.

   1. What kind of movie do you like best?
   2. What kind of movie do you like least?
   3. What is your favorite movie? Who are the stars of that movie? Who are the main characters? What type of movie is it? When and where does it take place?

Movie stills from *A Night at the Opera, Singing in the Rain,* and *The Maltese Falcon* courtesy MGM/Turner Entertainment Company.

Building Vocabulary

A. Circle the adjectives that describe your favorite movie.

exciting	interesting	entertaining
funny	realistic	action-packed
fascinating	sad	well-written, well-directed
informative	imaginative	frightening
horrifying	touching	heart-warming

B. Who is your favorite character in the movie? What is he or she like? **Circle the adjectives that describe him or her.**

crazy	talkative	loyal
funny	well-informed	smart
angry	shy	well-educated
evil	talented	interesting
fun-loving	ambitious	hard-working
brave	kind	successful

C. List any other adjectives that describe this character:

_____   _____   _____

_____   _____   _____

Organizing Ideas

Summarizing a Movie Plot

You are going to write a paragraph about your favorite movie.

A. In ten minutes, write the plot of your favorite movie. Write it as a list of events. Don't worry about grammar or form. If there are any words you don't know, write them in your native language.

B. Look at this list of events from the movie *The Wizard of Oz.*

1. Dorothy tries to run away from home.
2. A tornado carries her far away to a magical place.
3. She lands in Munchkinland.
4. She meets the Munchkins and a good witch named Glinda.
5. She tells them she wants to go home.
6. The Munchkins tell her to follow a yellow brick road to the Emerald City, where a wizard will help her.
7. Glinda gives her a pair of magical shoes.

The Wizard of Oz, courtesy MGM/Turner Entertainment Company

8. On her journey, she meets a scarecrow. He joins her to ask the wizard for a brain.
9. They meet a tin woodsman who goes with them to ask for a heart.
10. They meet a cowardly lion and take him along so he can ask the wizard for courage.
11. A bad witch puts them to sleep just as they approach the Emerald City.
12. They finally get to see the wizard.
13. The strange and frightening wizard tells them they must bring him the bad witch's broom before he will help them.
14. They go to the witch's castle.
15. The witch locks Dorothy up.
16. Her friends save her.
17. The witch sets the scarecrow on fire.
18. Dorothy throws water on the scarecrow, but misses him.
19. The water hits the bad witch and she melts.
20. They take the broom to the wizard.
21. They learn that the wizard is only an ordinary man.
22. The wizard shows the scarecrow, the tin woodsman, and the lion that they already have what they are looking for.
23. Glinda helps Dorothy see how important home really is.
24. Dorothy hits her heels (feet) together three times and says, "There's no place like home."
25. She wakes up in her own bed.
26. She discovers that her adventure was only a dream, but that she learned an important lesson.

C. A good movie summary should tell the reader the problem and the events that lead to the solution. Read these two summaries. Which is the better summary of the movie *The Wizard of Oz*? Why?

> Dorothy is lost. She keeps trying to find her way home. She meets the Munchkins. She meets a scarecrow, a tin woodsman, and a lion. A bad witch locks her up in a castle. Dorothy throws water on the witch, and the witch melts. She gives the wizard the witch's broom. The wizard is really an ordinary man. A good witch tells her how she can go home. She wakes up and realizes it was all a dream.

> The Wizard of Oz is the story of a young girl named Dorothy, who tries to run away from home. A tornado carries Dorothy off to a magical land. In this magical place, she meets many strange and wonderful characters, but Dorothy wants to get back home again. A scarecrow who wants a brain, a tin woodsman who wants a real heart, and a cowardly lion who wants courage all travel with her to the Emerald City to ask a great wizard for help. A bad witch tries to keep them from finding the wizard, while a good witch helps them on their journey. With the help of the wizard, who is really an ordinary man, and the good witch, they all learn important things about themselves, and they get what they are looking for. When Dorothy learns that home is the best place on earth, she is able to return. She realizes that her adventure was only a dream, but one with an important lesson.

D. Look back at the list of events you wrote from your favorite movie. Which events are the most important? Are there any sentences about events that you can combine?

Including Important Information in a Summary

The paragraph that you write should have more information than a summary of the events in the movie.

A. The paragraph that follows includes all of the information in the list below. Read the paragraph, find all the information listed, and write it on the lines.

1. the problem _____

2. where the movie takes place _____

3. the result _____

4. the main characters _____

5. when the movie takes place _____

6. the type of movie _____

<u>E.T.: The Extra-Terrestrial</u>:
A Heartwarming Adventure

One of my favorite movies is <u>E.T.: The Extra-Terrestrial</u>, a touching science-fiction story about the friendship of a young boy and a creature from outer space. It takes place in the 1980s in a small American town. When E.T.'s spaceship leaves without him, he meets Elliot, a boy who becomes his friend. E.T. likes Elliot, but he is very homesick, so Elliot decides to help him contact his friends. This is not easy because some scientists are searching for E.T. in order to study him. Elliot and E.T. escape from the scientists by bicycle. They go to the woods to meet the spaceship that will take E.T. home.

B. Look at your summary of your favorite movie. Make a list of any other information you would like to add.

Writing a Title

A. If you give your paragraph an interesting title, people will want to read it. Look at the following titles. Which movies would you like to read about?

1. <u>The Godfather</u>: My Favorite Movie
2. <u>E.T.</u>: An Unforgettable Experience
3. <u>The Wizard of Oz</u>: A Good Movie

B. Write a title for your paragraph.

PART TWO

DEVELOPING WRITING SKILLS

Developing Cohesion and Style

Using Adjectives

A. Look back at the list of adjectives that describe movies in the section "Building Vocabulary." Find appropriate adjectives to add to the following sentences.

1. Star Wars is a science-fiction movie. _____

   _____

2. Dracula is a horror movie about a vampire. _____

   _____

3. The Godfather is a drama about organized crime in the United States.

   _____

   _____

4. Gandhi is a drama about the life of the famous Indian leader. _____

   _____

B. Write a similar sentence about your favorite movie.

   _____

   _____

C. Look back at the list of adjectives that describe characters. Find appropriate adjectives to add to these sentences.

1. In the movie Star Wars, R2D2 is a robot. _____

   _____

2. E.T. is a visitor from another planet. _____

   _____

3. Sam Spade is a detective in the film The Maltese Falcon. _____

   _____

Sometimes you may want to use more than one adjective. You can separate two or more adjectives with a comma.

Examples: E.T. is a friendly, lovable creature from outer space.

In the movie *Rocky,* the main character is a handsome, determined boxer.

D. Look at these sentences. Put a comma between the two adjectives.

1. Gandhi is the story of a wise kind man who leads India to freedom.
2. In It's a Wonderful Life, James Stewart plays a hard-working ordinary man.
3. The 400 Blows tells the story of a lonely unhappy boy.
4. In the movie The Wizard of Oz, there is a mean frightening witch.

However, when there are two contrasting adjectives, you can separate them with *but*.

Example: In *Star Wars,* Han Solo is a brave *but* self-centered pilot.

E. Put the word *but* in the appropriate places in the sentences.

    1. <u>Gandhi</u> is about a gentle powerful leader.

    2. <u>Frankenstein</u> is the story of a destructive tragic monster.

    3. The Godfather is an evil loyal man.

    4. In <u>E.T.</u>, the boy Elliot is sensitive brave.

F. Write sentences that describe the main characters in your favorite movie. Use more than one adjective in each sentence.

Using Appositives

An appositive modifies a noun and follows it directly.

Example: Han Solo, *a brave but self-centered pilot,* is one of the heroes of *Star Wars.*

A. Can you find any appositives in the paragraph about *E.T.: The Extra-Terrestrial?* Underline them.

B. Combine the following sentences; use appositives.

    1. <u>Gone with the Wind</u> takes place in the South of the United States. It is a film about the U.S. Civil War. _____

    _____

    _____

    2. Elizabeth Taylor starred in <u>National Velvet.</u> She is a beautiful and talented actress. _____

    _____

    _____

    3. Han Solo needed help from R2D2. R2D2 was a robot. _____

    _____

    _____

    4. Steven Spielberg directed <u>Close Encounters of the Third Kind.</u> It is the story of an alien's visit to earth. _____

    _____

    _____

Using the Historical Present Tense

Look back at the paragraph about *E.T.: The Extra-Terrestrial*. What tense is it in? You can use the present tense to talk about events in the past. This is the "historical present." Look at the following paragraph and complete it with the correct forms of the verbs in parentheses. Use the historical present.

It's a Wonderful Life _____ (be) a heartwarming drama. In this movie, James Stewart _____ (play) an ordinary family man who _____ (live) in a small American town. When he is about to lose his business because of a serious mistake, Stewart _____ (become) very depressed. He _____ (try) to jump off a bridge, but an angel _____ (show) him how important he _____ (be) to his friends, family, and the community. He then _____ (decide) not to kill himself.

Using Correct Form

Punctuating Titles

Titles of movies are underlined (or put in italics in printed material). All the important words in a title (of a movie, book, etc.) begin with a capital letter. Small words such as *in, a, the, to, at,* or *with* do not begin with a capital letter unless they are the first words in the title.

Examples: The Adventures of Tarzan
                A Night at the Opera

Punctuate the titles in parentheses and capitalize words that need capital letters.

1. You should see (the seven samurai), a Japanese film.
2. The Mexican actor Cantinflas was in (around the world in eighty days).
3. The Marx brothers appeared in (a day at the races) and (the big store).
4. The most famous American movie is probably (gone with the wind), the story of Southern families during the Civil War.
5. I saw (the children of paradise) yesterday.

WRITING AND EDITING

Now write your paragraph about your favorite movie.

Editing Practice

Edit this paragraph twice and rewrite it correctly. The first time, take out any unnecessary details. The second time, make sure all of the remaining verbs are in the historical present. Make any other changes you think are necessary.

Star Trek II: The Wrath of Khan

Star Trek II is a science-fiction adventure film. In this movie, Khan, an evil clever leader stole information about Genesis, a secret government experiment. Leonard Nimoy played Mr. Spock. The crew of the spaceship Enterprise had to catch Khan before he could use the information. Captain Kirk and his crew succeeded as usual, but in the end, the captain lost a good friend. Which one of the crew died? See the movie and find out it's definitely a good film to watch. I liked this movie a lot. Maybe you will, too.

Editing Your Writing

Now edit the first draft of your summary. First exchange summaries with a partner and discuss your work. Then check your own for:

1. Content

    a. Is the title interesting?
    b. Would other people want to see the movie because of your summary?
    c. Did you present the information clearly?

2. Organization

    a. Are there any unnecessary details?
    b. Does the paragraph have an effective topic sentence?
    c. Does the paragraph have a good concluding sentence?

3. Cohesion and style

    Did you use appositives correctly?

Writing the Second Draft

A. After you edit your summary the first time, rewrite it neatly. Use good handwriting and correct form. Then check it for:

1. Grammar

    a. Are the verb tenses correct? Did you use the historical present tense?
    b. Are there any sentence fragments?

2. Form

    a. Does the title have correct punctuation and capitalization?
    b. Did you use commas correctly?

B. Discuss the corrections you made with other students.

PART FOUR

COMMUNICATING THROUGH WRITING

Give your paragraph to your teacher for comments.

Sharing

Read three of your classmates' movie summaries. Discuss which movies you would like to see and why.

Using Feedback

Look at your teacher's comments. If you don't understand something, ask about it. Then look at the paragraphs you wrote for the last three or four chapters. In what areas do you see improvement in your work? What areas still need more improvement?

Developing Your Skills

A. Find a review of a current movie in a newspaper or magazine. Bring it to class and discuss it. What information does the review include? Is it a good review? Does it make you want to see the movie?

B. With a partner, choose a current movie or television program you would both like to see. Watch it, then each of you can write a summary of it. Exchange summaries and compare them. Are they the same or different? Did your partner include information that you did not?

Developing Fluency

A. Write for fifteen minutes in your journal about why you (don't) go to the movies.

B. Write for fifteen minutes in your journal about what your favorite kind of movie is (for example, comedy, horror, drama, etc.) and why it is your favorite.

9

FRIENDS AND SOCIAL LIFE

GETTING READY TO WRITE

Exploring Ideas

Interviewing Someone

A. Look at these pictures of Tony, a foreign student studying English. Then describe Tony. What has he been doing during the past year? How has he been feeling? Use the information in the pictures and add other information. Write as many sentences as you can in ten minutes.

B. Discuss the kind of information you wrote in your sentences. Did you write about any of the following topics? What did you say about each topic?

- Family life
- Social life
- Work
- Accomplishments
- Unusual events

C. Write questions about the preceding topics. Think of other questions you could ask a student in your class. Your teacher will list them on the board.

D. Interview a student about his or her life in the past year. Take notes on the information your partner gives you.

Building Vocabulary

Add other words and expressions you used in your discussions and interview to the following list.

Nouns	Verbs	Adjectives	Other
accomplishment	accomplish	exhausted	_____
hobby	attend	fascinating	_____
recreation	_____	_____	_____
_____	_____	_____	_____
_____	_____	_____	_____
_____	_____	_____	_____
_____	_____	_____	_____

Organizing Ideas

You are going to write a paragraph about a student in your class for a class newsletter. The paragraph will tell you what the student has been doing for the past year.

Writing Topic Sentences

Topic sentences about what someone has been doing for the past year are often in the present perfect tense: *has* or *have* plus past participle.

A. Which of these sentences are good general topic sentences for a paragraph about Tony's life during the past year? Circle the numbers of those sentences. Which sentence do you think is the most interesting? Put a check by it.

1. Tony Prado has had a busy life this year.
2. Tony Prado has been married since June.
3. This year Tony Prado has had so much to do he has felt like a juggler.
4. Tony Prado has learned a lot of English this year.
5. During the past year Tony Prado has gotten married, worked at two jobs, played soccer, and studied English.
6. During the past year Tony Prado has had a full but happy life.

B. Write a topic sentence for your paragraph. Use the present perfect or present perfect continuous tense. _____

_____

Organizing Information in a Paragraph

There are several ways to organize your paragraph. Two ways are:

1. You can begin with more important activities such as work, and you can end with less important activities such as hobbies or interesting events.
2. You can begin with difficult activities and end with more enjoyable activities.

A. Look at the notes about Tony's life. Work in small groups and arrange them in order. Use one of the two types of organization above.

goes to English classes--has no time to study

works in uncle's factory--makes him tired

got married in June

rides bikes with his wife

works evenings in a beauty salon

plays soccer with friends

B. Look at your notes from your interview and arrange them in the order you think you are going to write about. Discuss the order with your partner.

Writing a Concluding Sentence

The final sentence of a paragraph sometimes summarizes the paragraph or leads into the future.

A. Look at these examples of possible final sentences.

1. In November Tony's wife is going to have a baby, and then he will have another thing to juggle in his busy schedule.
2. With her new English skills, Sonia is hoping to get a better job.
3. Parvin says that it's a full-time job to take care of her kids, but she can't wait till they are in school and she can get a job that pays money.
4. Satoshi is going to return to Japan and use his English in his engineering work.

B. Write a final sentence you could use in your paragraph. _____

_____

PART TWO

DEVELOPING WRITING SKILLS

Developing Cohesion and Style

Selecting the Correct Tense

It's important for each sentence to be in the correct tense. You can use this chart to check your verb tenses.

	Contrast of Verb Tenses
Simple present	A repeated or habitual action in the present.
	Example: Mina studies English in Austin, Texas.
Present continuous	An action or situation that is *in progress* in the present.
	Example: Mina is studying and working at the same time this quarter.
Future	An action or state that will occur in the future.
	Example: Mina will be in Texas for at least two years.
Past	A completed action or state.
	Example: Mina came to Austin three months ago.
Present perfect	An action or, more usually, a state (with verbs like *be, have, feel, know*) that began in the past and continues in the present. Often appears with *for* and *since* + time expression.
	Example: Mina has known her friend Salima since 1986; she has known her friend Sally for one month.
Present perfect continuous	An action that began in the past and continues in the present; often appears with *for* and *since* + time expression.
	Example: Mina has been working part time in the school cafeteria since she arrived (for three months).

A. Complete this paragraph with the correct tenses of the verbs in parentheses. Remember that you can use the present perfect or present perfect continuous to introduce a subject and then use the present tense to talk about it further.

This year Tony _____ ₁ (have) so much to do he

_____ ₂ (feel) like a juggler. He _____ ₃ (get)

married in June and he and his wife are very happy together. He

_____ ₄ (work) in his uncle's factory since April. It

_____ (be) hard work, because he _____ (have)
$\frac{}{5}$ $\frac{}{6}$

to load trucks and he _____ (get) very tired. In addition, he
$\frac{}{7}$

_____ (work) a few evenings a week as a hairdresser because
$\frac{}{8}$

he _____ (need) to save money. He also _____
$\frac{}{9}$ $\frac{}{10}$

(take) English classes at a community college near his home. He

_____ (enjoy) the class, but he _____ (be) so
$\frac{}{11}$ $\frac{}{12}$

busy he _____ (not have) much time to study. Tony's life
$\frac{}{13}$

_____ (not be) all work, however. In fact, he still
$\frac{}{14}$

_____ (find) time to enjoy a few sports. He
$\frac{}{15}$

_____ (play) soccer with some friends every Sunday. In
$\frac{}{16}$

addition, he and his wife often _____ (ride) bikes together.
$\frac{}{17}$

But she is pregnant now and _____ (have) a baby in four
$\frac{}{18}$

months. Then Tony _____ (have) another thing to juggle
$\frac{}{19}$

in his busy schedule.

B. Write five sentences from your interview notes. Underline each verb, then check to
see if you've used the correct tense.

Using Transitional Words and Phrases

However, in addition, also

The expressions *however, in addition,* and *also* help unify the sentences in a paragraph.

A. Find these expressions in the paragraph about Tony and underline them. Then
answer these questions.

   1. Which two expressions do you use when you give additional information?

   _____

   2. Which expression do you use when you give contrasting information?

   _____ In the paragraph about Tony, is this expression at the

   beginning or end of the sentence? _____ Can it be in another

   position? _____

In fact

You can use *in fact* to give facts that show that the sentence before is true.

Example: Tony has been very busy. *In fact,* he's been working at two jobs.

B. Add *in fact* or *however* to these sentences.

1. Tony has been working very hard. He works from 8:00 in the morning until 9:00 at night. _____

    _____

2. Tony has been working very hard. He still finds time to play soccer every week. _____

    _____

3. Ralph has been doing so well, and he likes his English class a lot. He's been studying so much that he isn't sleeping well. _____

    _____

    _____

4. Ralph has been doing well in his English class. He went from Level 2 to Level 4 last month. _____

    _____

C. Use the information in the pictures to make sentences with *in fact* or *however*.

1. Angela has been relaxing this summer. _____

    _____ every day.

2. Angela has been relaxing this summer. _____

_____ twice a week, too.

3. Khalil has been taking care of his children this summer. _____

_____ every afternoon.

4. Khalil has been taking care of his children this summer. _____

_____ every Saturday.

D. Look at your notes and write some pairs of sentences for your paragraph. Begin the second sentence of each pair with *in addition, also, however,* or *in fact.*

_____

_____

_____

_____

_____

_____

Stating Results with *so . . . that*

You can combine sentences giving reasons and results.

REASON		RESULT	
Tony has been busy.	+	He has felt like a juggler.	=

Tony has been *so* busy *that* he has felt like a juggler.

A. Combine these sentences using *so . . . that.*

1. Jane has been busy. She hasn't had much time to study. _____

    _____

2. Reiko was happy. She cried. _____

    _____

3. Chi Wang has been working hard. He falls asleep in class. _____

    _____

4. Nick has been having much fun. He is seldom homesick. _____

    _____

5. Sonia's daughter has been sick. She had to take her to the hospital. ___

    _____

    _____

B. Can you write any sentences with *so . . . that* for your paragraph? Write them here.

_____

_____

_____

_____

Using Correct Form

Using Commas with Transitional Words and Phrases

Commas separate *in addition, however,* and *in fact* from the rest of the sentence.

Examples: In fact, she won a skiing award.
                  She has not been practicing recently, however.

Do not use commas with *also* when it is in the middle of a sentence.

Example: She's also been skating a lot.

A. Add commas to these sentences if necessary.

1. Pierre has not been to New York yet however.
2. In fact he has been going to parties every weekend.
3. He has also been studying karate.
4. However he has met someone nice.
5. In fact they have been going out since August.
6. However she has been getting to know some of the other students in her class.

B. Check the punctuation in the sentences you wrote for Exercise D on page 112.

Using Long Forms in Formal Writing

When English speakers write formally, they don't use as many contractions as when they speak—instead, they use long forms. Here are some examples of contractions and their long forms:

he has → he's	he has not → he hasn't
they have → they've	they have not → they haven't
it is → it's	it is not → it's not, it isn't

Write these sentences without contractions.

1. He's been playing in a band. _____

2. They haven't moved yet. _____

3. They're not having problems with Canadian customs. _____

    _____

4. Recently she's been planning a party. _____

    _____

5. It's difficult work. _____

_____

6. She's been getting dates from a computer dating service. _____

_____

Spelling Present and Past Participles Correctly

Write the *-ing* form and the past participle of these words. For rules for adding *-ing,* see Appendix 1 at the back of this book.

		-ing FORM	PAST PARTICIPLE
1.	work	*working*	*worked*
2.	begin	_____	_____
3.	study	_____	_____
4.	make	_____	_____
5.	find	_____	_____
6.	swim	_____	_____
7.	go	_____	_____
8.	travel	_____	_____
9.	come	_____	_____
10.	have	_____	_____

Using Correct Capitalization

In your paragraph, remember to capitalize time words correctly. (See Appendix 2 for detailed rules.)

Capitalize months and days of the week.

     July   September   Monday   September

Don't capitalize seasons.

     summer   fall   winter   spring

Capitalize names of schools and businesses.

     Lincoln Community College   Lucia's Bakery
     University of Montreal   Internet, Inc.

Don't capitalize kinds of schools, businesses, or jobs.

     a bakery   a baker
     an export company   an accountant
     a community college   a musician

Don't capitalize school subjects except languages.

business math   French
biology   English

Write these sentences with correct capitalization.

1. Pablo has been studying computer science and english at northwest-
   ern college since january. _____

   _____

2. Anna works as a dietician at randolph college. _____

   _____

3. In september Van got a job as a mail clerk at a bank. _____

   _____

4. Tessa has been studying fashion design every tuesday and thursday
   evening. _____

   _____

5. Irena has been working with the jones plumbing company since the
   fall. _____

   _____

WRITING AND EDITING

Writing the First Draft

Now write your paragraph about a classmate. Use your topic sentence and notes. Also use transitional expressions to unify your paragraph.

Editing Practice

Edit this paragraph twice and rewrite it correctly. The first time, see if the ideas are well organized. Do you need to rearrange any sentences? The second time, correct any problems with verb tenses and form. Make any other changes you think are necessary.

Marta Duarte has have a very interesting year. Last June she graduated from a tourism development course in Mexico. She received a scholarship to study English and has been attending classes here at the University of Ottawa since September. marta is twenty-five years old. She's also been traveling in Canada and the United States. She love dance and goes dancing at least two nights a week. She visits hotels to study the different management systems and has learned a lot. In fact, she says that one day in a hotel is better than ten days in a classroom. However, Marta hasn't spend all her time in Canada at work. She also find time to develop a close friendship with the manager of a big hotel here in Ottawa. She is hoping to get to know him better.

Editing Your Writing

Now edit the paragraph you wrote. Check it for:

1. Content

    a. Is the information interesting?
    b. Is all the information in the paragraph important?

2. Organization

    a. Does the topic sentence give the main idea of the paragraph?
    b. Are the sentences well organized?
    c. Does the paragraph have a good concluding sentence?

3. Cohesion and style

    a. Did you use transitional expressions correctly?
    b. Did you use *so . . . that* correctly?
    c. Did you use long forms rather than contractions as appropriate?

Writing the Second Draft

A. After you edit your paragraph the first time, rewrite it neatly. Use good handwriting and correct form. Then check it for:

1. Grammar

    Did you use correct verb forms?

2. Form

    a. Did you use commas correctly?
    b. Did you spell the verb forms correctly?
    c. Did you use correct capitalization?

B. Discuss the corrections you made with other students.

PART FOUR

COMMUNICATING THROUGH WRITING

Give your paragraph to your teacher for comments.

Sharing

As a class, collect all the paragraphs you wrote to make a class newsletter.

Using Feedback

Look at your teacher's comments. If you don't understand something, ask about it. Then discuss these questions.

1. What have you learned in your writing class?
2. How do you feel about writing now? Do you enjoy it? Do you think it's difficult?
3. Which step of the writing process do you like? Which step don't you like?
4. What do you think you need to practice more?
5. Have you found anything that makes writing easier for you? Tell the rest of the class about it.
6. Is there anything you would like to change in the writing class? What is it?
7. Are you doing enough writing? Would you like to do more or less?

Developing Your Skills

A. Write a paragraph about what you have been doing in the last year.

B. Write a paragraph about what you *want* to do in the next year.

Developing Fluency

Write in your journal for as long as you want about anything you like.

10

CUSTOMS, CELEBRATIONS, AND HOLIDAYS

GETTING READY TO WRITE

Exploring Ideas

Describing Holidays

A. Look at the photographs and discuss them. What do you know about the holidays the people in the photos are celebrating?

B. What are the most important holidays in your country or culture? When do people celebrate these holidays? How do they celebrate them? Complete the following chart.

Christmas

Carnival, Brazil

Chinese New Year

Eid al-Adha (Moslem Feast of the Sacrifice)

HOLIDAY	TIME OF YEAR	ACTIVITIES	DESCRIPTION OF ACTIVITIES

C. Look at your list of holidays. How could you divide them into groups? Try dividing them by seasons first (winter holidays, summer holidays, etc.).

_____

_____

_____

_____

_____

_____

_____

_____

_____

D. Suggest other ways to group them (by activity, purpose, etc.).

_____

_____

_____

_____

_____

_____

_____

Building Vocabulary

Add words you used to describe holidays to this list.

Nouns	Verbs	Adjectives	Other
celebration	celebrate	traditional	_____
commemoration	commemorate	joyous	_____
parade	_____	_____	_____
fireworks	_____	_____	_____
tradition	_____	_____	_____
_____	_____	_____	_____
_____	_____	_____	_____
_____	_____	_____	_____

Organizing Ideas

You are going to write a paragraph about holidays in your culture.

Categorizing and Making an Outline

Here is an example of the notes that a North American student made about holidays in her country.

Christmas	Washington's Birthday	Halloween
New Year's	Valentine's Day	Easter
Thanksgiving	Memorial Day	Passover
July 4	Labor Day	Rosh Hashana

She decided to divide the holidays into three categories.

1. political holidays
2. religious holidays
3. traditional holidays

Some people feel that it is easier to organize their ideas in outline form. Before the student began to write her paragraph, she made an outline like this:

I. Holidays in the United States

    A. Political holidays

        1. Independence Day

        2. Presidents' Day

        3. Memorial Day

        4. Labor Day

B. Traditional holidays

   1. Thanksgiving

   2. New Year's

   3. Halloween

   4. Valentine's Day

C. Religious holidays

   1. Christian holidays

      a. Christmas

      b. Easter

   2. Jewish holidays

      a. Passover

      b. Rosh Hashana

A. Does your country have any political holidays? Traditional holidays? Religious holidays? Make an outline like the one the student from the United States made.

The North American student decided to write about political holidays, so she added more information to her outline. Here is her outline; some of the items are missing.

I. Holidays in the United States

  A. Political holidays

    1. Independence Day

      a. Fourth of July

      b. _____

      c. Picnics, barbecues

      d. Fireworks

    2. _____

      a. Commemorate the American soldiers who died in all wars

      b. Parades

      c. Put flags and flowers on graves

      d. Last weekend in May

      e. _____

    3. Labor Day

      a. _____

      b. Honor American workers

Fourth of July parade

    c. Parades

    d. Picnics, beach

    e. _____

4. _____

    a. George Washington

    b. _____

    c. Martin Luther King, Jr.

B. Read this paragraph. Then fill in the outline that the North American student made with the information that is missing.

Holidays in the United States

There are three types of holidays in the United States: political holidays, traditional holidays, and religious holidays. There are more political holidays than any other type. The most important political holiday is Independence Day, the Fourth of July. On this day we celebrate our independence from Great Britain. Most people spend the day with their family and friends. Picnics and barbecues are very popular. In addition, almost every city and town has a fireworks display at night. Another very important political holiday is Memorial Day. On this holiday we commemorate all the soldiers who died for our country. Many towns and cities have parades, and some people go to cemeteries and put flowers or flags on the soldiers' graves. Because this holiday falls on the last weekend in May, some people think of it as the beginning of the summer season. A third important political holiday is Labor Day, which we celebrate on the first Monday in September. This is the day when we honor the workers of the United States. People watch parades, go on picnics, or go to the beach. For students, Labor Day is a bittersweet holiday, because when it is over they must begin school again. Besides these political holidays, we also celebrate the birthdays of George Washington, Abraham Lincoln, and Martin Luther King, Jr.

Ordering Information According to Importance

A. When you make a list, you usually put the items in order of importance. Look back at the preceding paragraph. What is the most important political holiday?

B. Here is part of an outline a student made about holidays in the United States. It shows the order of importance of traditional holidays. Can you explain why she chose this order?

   B. Traditional holidays
      1. Thanksgiving
         a. Third Thursday in November
         b. People feel thankful for the good things in their lives
         c. Families eat turkey and other traditional foods
      2. New Year's Day
         a. January 1
         b. People celebrate the New Year
      3. Halloween
         a. October 31
         b. Children dress in costumes
         c. People go to costume parties
         d. Children collect candy
      4. Valentine's Day
         a. February 14
         b. Boys and girls exchange valentines

Notice that 1.a., 2.a., 3.a., and 4.a all have the same *type* of information.

C. Look at your list of holidays. Make an outline about traditional holidays in your country or culture, showing the order of importance. Use as many spaces to write in as you need.

B. *Traditional holidays* _____

1. _____
     a. _____
     b. _____

2. _____
     a. _____
     b. _____

3. _____
     a. _____
     b. _____
     c. _____
     d. _____

4. _____
     a. _____
     b. _____
     c. _____

D. Make an outline for the type of holiday you are going to write about.

PART TWO

DEVELOPING WRITING SKILLS

Developing Cohesion and Style

Listing Information with *in addition to, besides, another,* and *the first, second, third, last*

You can use these transitional words to add information: *in addition to, besides, another,* and *the first, second, third, last.*

A. Look at the paragraph about holidays in the United States on page 123. Underline the transitional words that are for adding information.

B. The following paragraph contains no transitional words. Complete it with the appropriate transitions. More than one answer may be correct.

    Salvadorans celebrate several political holidays each year. The most important one is Independence Day on September 15. On this day, people parade in the streets, sing songs, and recite poems. _____₁ important political holiday is Labor Day. Labor Day is the first day in May. _____₂ Labor Day and Independence Day, Salvadorans also celebrate the birthday of José Matías Delgado, the "father of the country." _____₃ these holidays, there are other minor holidays such as el *Día de la Raza.*

Unifying a Paragraph with Pronouns and Pronominal Expressions

You can use pronouns to refer to things you have already mentioned so that you don't have to repeat the same words again and again.

A. Here is a list of the pronouns and pronominal expressions in the paragraph about holidays in the United States. Tell what each one refers to.

1. on this day (line 4) _____

2. on this holiday (line 8) _____

3. this holiday (line 11) _____

4. it (line 12) _____

5. this is the day (line 14) _____

6. it (line 16) _____

7. they (line 16) _____

B. The paragraph that follows needs more pronouns. Edit it and substitute pronouns or pronominal expressions for *some* of the nouns. Remember that too many pronouns are as bad as too few.

    Americans celebrate several traditional holidays. One traditional holiday Americans celebrate is New Year's. Americans often go to parties and drink champagne on New Year's Eve. In addition, Americans sometimes wear silly hats and blow horns. At midnight, Americans kiss the person next to them and wish everyone a happy new year at New Year's Eve parties.

Using Quantifiers

For a paragraph like the one you are going to write, you will probably need to use quantifiers, words that tell the amount of something. Some quantifiers are:

many			much		
some			some		
a few	+ count noun		most	+ noncount noun	
most			a lot of		
a lot of			a little		
all			all		

How many quantifiers can you find in the paragraph about holidays in the United States? Underline them.

Using Nonrestrictive Relative Clauses

In Chapter 7 you learned about restrictive relative clauses with *who* and *that.*

Examples: Ramadan is the Moslem holiday *that lasts a month.*
Moslems *who celebrate Ramadan* fast (do not eat) from sunrise to sunset during this month.

A restrictive relative clause tells you which person or thing the writer is referring to. A nonrestrictive relative clause gives additional information. This information is not necessary. You can omit a nonrestrictive relative clause, but you cannot omit a restrictive relative clause.

Examples: Thanksgiving, *which falls in November,* is a time for families to get together. (nonrestrictive)
Notice that you can omit the clause *which falls in November: Thanksgiving is a time for families to get together.*
Christmas is the holiday *that I like best.* (restrictive)
Notice that if you omit the clause *that I like best,* the sentence seems incomplete: *Christmas is the holiday.*

In nonrestrictive relative clauses, use *which* instead of *that.*

A. Combine these sentences with *which* and a nonrestrictive relative clause. Insert a clause at the ∧ mark.

1. Easter ∧ is a happy holiday. Easter comes in the springtime. _____

_____

_____

2. The Fourth of July ∧ is a time for big parades and fireworks. The Fourth of July is Independence Day. _____

_____

_____

3. Martin Luther King Day ∧ comes in January. Martin Luther King Day is our newest holiday. _____

_____

4. Halloween ∧ is a favorite children's holiday. Halloween is an ancient British tradition. _____

_____

_____

5. On New Year's Day ∧ there is a famous parade in Pasadena, California. New Year's Day is the first holiday of the year. _____

_____

_____

B. Write three sentences using nonrestrictive relative clauses about the holiday in your outline.

Using Correct Form

Punctuating Nonrestrictive Relative Clauses

Use commas to separate a nonrestrictive clause from the rest of the sentence. If the clause comes in the middle of the sentence, use two commas.

Example: Valentine's Day, which falls on February 14, is a holiday for lovers.

If the clause comes at the end of the sentence, use only one comma.

Example: Memorial Day is in May, which is almost the beginning of the summer in the United States.

A. Add commas where necessary in these sentences.

1. Songkran which is the Thai New Year is on April 13.
2. Eid-e-Ghorbon is a religious holiday in Iran which is a Muslim country.
3. Christmas which is an important holiday in Christian countries is usually a happy time.
4. Bastille Day which is on July 14 is a very important holiday in France.

B. Check the punctuation in the sentences you wrote in Exercise B above.

PART THREE

WRITING AND EDITING

Writing the First Draft

Now write your paragraph about holidays in your culture.

Editing Practice

Edit this paragraph twice and rewrite it correctly. The first time, check to see if the order of ideas is correct. (See the outline on page 124 if you need help.) The second time, check to see if the writer has used quantifiers correctly. Make any other changes you think are necessary.

<u>Traditional Holidays in the United States</u>

There are four important traditional holidays in the United States. Another important traditional holiday is New Year's. On New Year's Eve, most people go to parties. At twelve o'clock, everyone shouts "Happy New Year!" and they wish their friends good luck. New Year's parties usually last a long time. Some people don't go home until morning. The most important of these holidays is Thanksgiving, which we celebrate on the third Thursday in November. This is a family holiday. Most of people spend the day with their relatives. They feel thankful for the good things in their lives. The most important tradition on this day is Thanksgiving dinner. At a traditional Thanksgiving dinner, the most people eat turkey with stuffing, cranberry sauce, and pumpkin pie. The third traditional holiday, Halloween, is mainly for children. On this holiday, people dress as witches, ghosts, or other such

Children in Halloween costumes

things. Much of the children go from house to house and say "Trick or treat." If the people at the house do not give them candy, the children will play a trick on them. But this hardly ever happens. A most give them candy or fruit. Another holiday is Valentine's Day, which is in February. On this day, boys and girls exchange valentines, and men and women give each other cards, flowers, or candy.

Editing Your Writing

Now look at your paragraph. Check it for:

1. Content

    a. Is the information interesting?
    b. Is there enough information?

2. Organization

    a. Did you list the holidays from most important to least important?
    b. Did you give the same type of information about each holiday?

3. Cohesion and style

    a. Did you use expressions such as *in addition to, besides, another, the first (second, etc.)*?
    b. Did you use quantifiers correctly?
    c. Did you use pronouns and pronominal expressions appropriately?
    d. Did you use relative clauses correctly?

Writing the Second Draft

A. After you edit your paragraph the first time, rewrite it neatly. Use good handwriting and correct form. Then check it for:

1. Grammar

    a. Are the verb forms correct?
    b. Are there any sentence fragments?

2. Form

    Do the relative clauses have commas where necessary?

B. Discuss the corrections you made with other students.

PART FOUR

COMMUNICATING THROUGH WRITING

Give your paragraph to your teacher for comments.

Sharing

Bring in pictures to illustrate different holidays your class celebrates. Put them on a bulletin board.

Using Feedback

Look at your teacher's comments. If you don't understand something, ask about it. Then compare your first draft and your second draft. What mistakes were easy for you to find? What mistakes did you miss? Make a list of the kinds of mistakes you need to avoid.

Developing Your Skills

A. Write a paragraph about your favorite holiday. Explain why it is your favorite.

B. Interview a classmate about his or her favorite holiday. In a paragraph, explain why it is his or her favorite.

Developing Fluency

A. Write in your journal for fifteen minutes about what you miss the most from your country or culture.

B. Write in your journal for as long as you want about anything you like.

RECREATION

GETTING READY TO WRITE

Exploring Ideas

Describing Recreational Activities

A. Look at the picture of the park and write as much as you can about it in five minutes. Tell what the people are doing and what has happened.

B. Discuss the picture. Answer these questions.

1. What are the people in the picture doing?
2. Which of the activities do you like to participate in?
3. Which of the activities do you like to watch?
4. What other things do you like to do in your free time?

C. Complete the following list about things you like to do.

OUTDOOR ACTIVITIES	INDOOR ACTIVITIES	ACTIVITIES YOU LIKE TO DO ALONE
_____	_____	_____
_____	_____	_____
_____	_____	_____
_____	_____	_____

ACTIVITIES YOU LIKE TO DO WITH OTHERS	ACTIVITIES YOU LIKE TO PARTICIPATE IN	ACTIVITIES YOU LIKE TO WATCH
_____	_____	_____
_____	_____	_____
_____	_____	_____
_____	_____	_____

D. Compare your list with those of some other students. Which activities are you most interested in? Which activities are they most interested in? Which activity would you like to recommend to other students?

Building Vocabulary

A. Add other words you used in your discussion to this list.

Nouns	Verbs	Adjectives	Other
roller skating	roller-skate	thrilling	_____
soccer	play (soccer)	relaxing	_____
spectator	listen to (music)	fun	_____
jazz band	participate in	exciting	_____
kite	benefit	enjoyable	_____
dominoes	stroll	peaceful	_____
benefit	_____	entertaining	_____
fun	_____	pleasant	_____
_____	_____	inexpensive	_____
_____	_____	spectacular	_____
_____	_____	sensational	_____
_____	_____	easy	_____
_____	_____	_____	_____
_____	_____	_____	_____
_____	_____	_____	_____

B. Tell what each of the words in the adjectives column means. Can you add other adjectives to the list?

Organizing Ideas

Organizing Information by Answering "What?," "Who?," "Where?," "When?," "How?," and "Why?"

You are going to write a paragraph about an activity you like and want to recommend to your classmates. One way to get ideas for your paragraph is to ask "What?," "Who?," "Where?," "When?," "How?," and "Why?" about your activity. This also gives you a way to order your ideas in your paragraph. For example, *what* the activity is should come first; it's the most important idea.

A. Look at how one student answered the six questions for the topic she chose.

ROLLER SKATING

1. What activity do you want to recommend? *roller skating*

2. Who can participate in this activity? *People of any age. Many families like to roller skate together. Young people often skate.*

3. Where can they do it? *Outdoors in parks or on the street, indoors in rinks*

4. When can they do it? *Day or evening.*

5. How can they do it? *Can rent skates in parks or indoor rinks. If they do it often, they can buy skates.*

6. Why would they like to do it? *It's an easy sport to learn. You can do it alone or with other people. It's fun to do to music. Not expensive. Good exercise.*

B. Answer the questions about the activity you are going to write about.

1. What activity do you recommend? _____

2. Who can participate in this activity? _____

   _____

3. Where can they do it? _____

   _____

   _____

4. When can they do it? _____

5. How can they do it? _____

   _____

   _____

6. Why would they like to do it? _____

   _____

   _____

Writing Topic Sentences

In a paragraph where you make a recommendation, you want the topic sentence to interest the reader in what you're going to say.

A. Look at these topic sentences for a paragraph recommending roller skating. Notice that sometimes the writer needed two sentences to get the reader's attention. Which topic sentences do you like? Why do you like them?

1. Roller skating used to be just for kids, but now thousands of adults are finding that it is a great sport.
2. Would you like to try a sport that is easy to learn, a lot of fun, and not expensive? Then roller skating may be for you.
3. Roller skating is a nice sport.
4. One of the most exciting feelings in the world is gliding through the park on a sunny day on roller skates.
5. I like to roller-skate because it is fun.
6. If you want to try a sport that's great for the whole family, then you may want to try roller-skating.

There are certain structures that commonly appear in topic sentences that try to interest the reader in the paragraph:

One of the most _____ I've ever _____ is _____ .

One of the most _____ in the world is _____ .

If you want _____ , then _____ .

Would you like _____ ? Then _____ .

B. Read this paragraph and then write four different topic sentences using the preceding structures.

The Benefits of Walking

_____ . Walking may not seem fascinating, but it can be. When you walk, you move slowly, so you can see the world around you. Walking is great because you can do it anytime and anywhere. An evening walk through the streets of a big city can be just as enjoyable as a morning stroll on a country road or a hike in the mountains. In addition, you don't need any fancy equipment to participate in this activity. If you have a good pair of shoes, you're ready to go. Another benefit of this pastime is that you can enjoy it with friends or alone. You also don't have to worry about winning or losing. Just getting there is enough.

Topic sentences:

1. _____
   _____

2. _____
   _____

3. _____
   _____

4. _____
   _____

C. Write a topic sentence or sentences that will interest a reader in the activity you are going to write about. You can use the preceding structures or think of another way to get the reader's interest.

_____

_____

PART TWO

DEVELOPING WRITING SKILLS

Developing Cohesion and Style

Unifying a Paragraph with Synonyms and Pronouns

One way of unifying a paragraph is to refer to the same word or topic several times. Sometimes you use the same word for the topic, and sometimes you use synonyms or other words to refer to it.

A. Find these words in the paragraph about walking and underline them.

it	this pastime	a morning stroll
this activity	an evening walk	

B. Insert these words into the paragraph that follows, "Dancing to Music":

roller skating	this activity
this sport	it

Follow these directions:

1. Don't repeat *roller skating* in the same sentence. Use *it* or *this sport/activity* the second time.
2. If you haven't used the term *roller skating* in a few sentences, repeat it.

Dancing to Music

One of the most exciting feelings in the world is gliding through the park on a sunny day on roller skates. People of any age can participate in _____ . Many families like to roller-skate together, and

$\underline{\qquad}_{1}$

_____ is the perfect activity for students who want to feel free

$\underline{\qquad}_{2}$

after a long day in the classroom. Another benefit of _____ is that

$\underline{\qquad}_{3}$

you can do _____ in an indoor rink or on the sidewalks of a park.

$\underline{\qquad}_{4}$

If you want to try _____ before buying skates, you can rent them

$\underline{\qquad}_{5}$

in rinks or stands near parks. _____ is an easy sport to learn. You

$\underline{\qquad}_{6}$

can do it alone or with friends. _____ is also not expensive and

$\underline{\qquad}_{7}$

_____ is good exercise. But the thing I like best about _____

$\underline{\qquad}_{8}$ $\underline{\qquad}_{9}$

is that you can skate to music. _____ is like dancing on wheels.

$\underline{\qquad}_{10}$

Using Gerunds

When writing about recreational activities, you can use gerunds as subjects, objects, and objects of prepositions.

Examples: *Roller skating* is easy to learn. (subject)
I enjoy *walking*. (object)
You can try it before *buying* skates. (object of preposition)

A. Find the gerunds in the paragraph above and in the one about walking. Tell whether they are subjects, objects, or objects of prepositions. Does a singular or plural verb follow the subjects?

B. Complete these sentences with gerund phrases.

1. _____ is one of the most exciting sports I've ever watched.

2. After _____ it feels great to take a hot shower.

3. I don't enjoy _____ .

4. Every weekend I look forward to _____ .

5. One of the benefits of _____ is that it's good exercise.

6. I've often dreamed of _____ .

7. Have you ever tried _____ ?

8. Last month he started _____ .

Using the Pronoun *you*

In informal writing English speakers often use the pronoun *you* when talking about people in general.

Examples: *You* can do this activity indoors or outdoors.
I'm sure *you* will find that parachuting is exciting.

Circle all the uses of the pronoun *you* in the paragraphs about walking and roller skating. Then write a few sentences for your paragraph using *you* to refer to people in general.

Using Adjectives + Infinitive Complements

When talking about recreational activities, you can use an adjective + *to* + a verb.

Examples: It's *necessary to use* the correct equipment for American football.
Volleyball is *easy to learn*.

Make at least six sentences with these adjectives and appropriate activities.

Example: It's easy to learn to play volleyball.

1. easy   a. play soccer
2. fun   b. watch baseball
3. exciting   c. learn to play table tennis
4. relaxing   d. listen to rock music
5. difficult   e. ride bicycles
6. enjoyable   f. learn to roller-skate

_____

_____

_____

_____

_____

_____

_____

_____

Using Correct Form

Forming the Superlative of Adjectives

Remember to add *-est* to most one-syllable adjectives and to adjectives ending in *-y*. Use *most* to form the superlative of other adjectives. For rules on the spelling of adjectives with *-est,* see Appendix 1 at the back of this book.

Examples: big → biggest   easy → easiest
            spectacular → most spectacular

A. Write the superlative of these words with *the.*

     Example: popular   *the most popular*

     1. nice   _____

     2. exciting   _____

     3. good   _____

     4. fascinating   _____

     5. relaxing   _____

     6. enjoyable   _____

     7. thrilling   _____

     8. cheap   _____

B. Write three sentences about the activity you chose using superlatives.

WRITING AND EDITING

Writing the First Draft

Now write your paragraph about a favorite activity. Use the notes and topic sentence you have written. Look at the titles of the paragraphs on walking and roller skating. Write an interesting title for your paragraph.

Editing Practice

Edit this paragraph twice and rewrite it correctly. The first time, check to see if the paragraph answers the questions "What?," "Who?," "Where?," "When?," "How?," and "Why?" The second time, check to see if the writer has used gerunds and adjectives + infinitive complements correctly. Make any other changes you think are necessary.

Mind Travel

If you would like to learn the most interesting, the most fun, and the most fascinating activity in the world, try daydreaming, the lazy person's sport. You can visit distant lands, win games, and meet interesting people, all in the comfort of your own home. You don't need any special equipment daydreaming. With just a good imagination, you are ready to beginning. Is easy learning. It is best to do it with closed eyes, but I have had many successful daydreams in crowded classrooms with my eyes wide open. Daydream is also fun while you are walking, riding the bus, or listening to boring stories. Group daydream is enjoyable, too. One person can begin a story and the others can add to it. If you start tomorrow, you will have years of excitement ahead of you.

Editing Your Writing

Now edit the paragraph you wrote. Check it for:

1. Content
   a. Is the paragraph interesting?
   b. Does the paragraph give good reasons for participating in the activity?

2. Organization

   a. Does the paragraph answer the questions "What?," "Who?," "Where?," "When?," "How?," and "Why?"
   b. Is there a good topic sentence to interest the reader in the paragraph?

3. Cohesion and style

   a. Did you repeat the name of the activity and refer to it with the pronoun *it* or *this* appropriately?
   b. Did you use the pronoun *you* to refer to people in general? (This is not essential, but it can be useful in writing this kind of paragraph.)

Writing the Second Draft

A. After you edit your paragraph the first time, rewrite it neatly. Then check it for:

1. Grammar

   a. Did you use adjectives + infinitive complements correctly?
   b. Did you use gerunds correctly?

2. Form

   Did you use correct superlative forms?

B. Discuss the corrections you made with other students.

PART FOUR

COMMUNICATING THROUGH WRITING

Give your paragraph to your teacher for comments.

Sharing

Some students can read their paragraphs aloud for the class. Are there any activities that interest many of the students? Would the class like to plan a class trip or activity based on the recommendations?

Using Feedback

Look at your teacher's comments. If you don't understand something, ask about it.

Read another student's paragraph and write two or three sentences about it. Tell why you thought it was interesting and write why you would or wouldn't like to participate in this activity.

Developing Your Skills

A. As a class, interview your teacher on his or her favorite free-time activity. Write a class paragraph on the board about your teacher's activity.

B. Write a paragraph about a recreational activity that you do in your home country but cannot do here. Explain why.

Developing Fluency

A. Write in your journal for fifteen minutes. Describe your favorite daydream.

B. Write in your journal for fifteen minutes on anything you like.

12

YOU, THE CONSUMER

GETTING READY TO WRITE

Exploring Ideas

Discussing Consumer Problems and Complaints

A. Look at these pictures, which show people who have just bought something that they are not happy with. What's wrong in each picture?

B. Discuss these questions in small groups.

1. Have you ever bought something from a store and been disappointed with it? What was the item? What was wrong with it?
2. What did you do? Did you keep the item? Did you take it back? If you took it back, what happened?

Building Vocabulary

Add other words you used in your discussion to this list.

Nouns	Verbs	Adjectives	Other
refund	refund	defective	
receipt	exchange	dissatisfied	
guarantee	return	guaranteed	
warranty	complain		
complaint department	purchase		
manager			

Organizing Ideas

Determining the Characteristics of an Effective Letter of Complaint

You are going to write a letter of complaint about something that you bought that you are dissatisfied with.

The well-written letter of complaint should:

1. state the problem clearly and simply
2. give definite dates, order numbers, etc.
3. suggest a solution
4. be polite
5. be addressed to the person who will be able to do something about the problem

A. Jaime Flores bought a kitchen appliance from a mail order catalog. Read his letter of complaint. Where does he need to add details?

Dear Sir,

 The other day I ordered an electric frying pan from your catalog. When it arrived, it didn't work. Please refund my money.

Sincerely,

Jaime Flores

Jaime Flores

Although it is important to include enough information, you should be careful *not* to include unnecessary details.

B. Marie Wolpert bought a suitcase at a large department store. She is unhappy with it and would like to return it. Here are notes for a letter that she is writing to the department manager. Read them and draw a line through any unnecessary details.

1. Skyway suitcase
2. 30″ × 45″
3. light blue
4. purchased June 17
5. paid cash
6. reduced from $50 to $42
7. handle broke on trip to Buffalo
8. handle broke first time used
9. called the store
10. spoke with the manager of luggage department on July 15

11. manager said no refunds or exchanges on sale items
12. manager's name Simon Grey
13. would like to exchange suitcase

C. Think of a time when you bought something that you were dissatisfied with. Make a list of the important details.

_____

_____

_____

_____

_____

_____

_____

_____

_____

_____

_____

_____

_____

D. Exchange lists with another student in your class. Can you understand the situation? Has he or she included all the important information? Has he or she included any unnecessary details?

PART TWO

DEVELOPING WRITING SKILLS

Developing Cohesion and Style

Using Past Participles as Adjectives

Many adjectives are the same as the past participle of a verb. Look at these sentences:

Examples: When the bowl arrived, it was *broken*. (past participle that functions as an adjective)
Oh no! I've *broken* the bowl! (past participle that is part of the present perfect tense: *have broken*)

A. Look at these verbs and tell what their past participles are. Then use the past participles as adjectives in a sentence.

Example: stain *stained*

The blouse looks stained with tomato juice.

1. smash _____

_____

2. open _____

_____

3. destroy _____

_____

4. tear _____

_____

5. fade _____

_____

6. dissatisfy _____

_____

7. rip _____

_____

8. scratch _____

_____

B. Look at the notes you made in Part One, Exercise C. Write five sentences about your complaint using past participles as adjectives.

Using Formal Language

A business letter should be formal and polite. People generally use more formal vocabulary in business letters than in letters to friends.

A. Here are some more formal alternatives for words you already know. Read the sentences and try to guess what the italicized words mean.

1. On May 12, I *purchased* a pair of shoes at your store.
2. I have been waiting for a refund for three weeks, but I haven't *received* it yet.
3. Therefore, I am *requesting* a refund.

To make a business letter polite, you should try not to be too direct. For example, instead of "You should refund my money," you might say, "I feel that the company should refund my money."

Another way to make a business letter more polite is to use the words *would* and *could* when you are making a request. Instead of "Please return my deposit," you might say, "Would (Could) you please return my deposit?" or "I would appreciate it if you would return my deposit."

B. Look at the following letter of complaint. Rewrite it to make it more formal and more polite.

Dear Sir,

Last week I bought a set of six glasses in your store. You sent them to my home. When I got the package, four of the glasses were broken. I want a refund for all six glasses. Send it to me soon.

Sincerely,

Kate Collins
Kate Collins

_____

_____

_____

_____

_____

_____

_____

_____

_____

_____

Using Correct Form

Following the Format of a Business Letter

A. Look at the business letter below.

HEADING ⎰	15 South Cedar Street
	Boston, Massachusetts 02214
⎱	January 11, 19XX

Manager
Sales Department
Universal Publishing Company   } **INSIDE ADDRESS**
1523 Castleton Boulevard
New York, New York 10027

Dear Sir: **SALUTATION**

On December 15, 19XX I ordered one copy of <u>The United</u>
<u>States in Pictures</u> by Jerome Massanti. I included a check for the
full price of the book, $18.97 plus $2.00 for shipping and
handling charges. On December 27 of last year I received a letter
from your order department that said that the book would not be
available until May of this year. The letter also said that if I
wanted a refund, I could have it. On January 2 I wrote and asked
them to refund my $20.97. It is now four weeks later and I still
have not received my refund.

BODY

Would you please look into this matter for me? I have often
ordered books from your company and would like to continue
doing business with you.

CLOSING ⟶ Very truly yours,

Simon La Grande

SIGNATURE ⟶ Simon La Grande

A business letter should contain all of the following elements:

HEADING: The heading tells where and when the writer wrote the letter. It should be in
the upper right-hand corner of the first page, an inch or more from the top. The heading should contain the date. It should also include the writer's complete address:

number and street
city, state or province, postal code
country (if the letter is sent out of the country)

INSIDE ADDRESS: The inside address contains the name and the address of the person or company you are writing to. It is usually on the left two spaces below the date. If you know the name and title of the person, you should include them. For example:

David Pearson, Manager
Sales Department

Margaret McGraw, Customer Relations

SALUTATION: The salutation or greeting should be two spaces below the inside address. The most common salutations are:

Dear Sir or Madam: Dear Ms. Kaplan:
Dear Mr. Fraser: Dear Mrs. Foster:

BODY: The body of the letter begins two spaces below the salutation. You should indent the paragraphs. There should be a margin of at least one inch on both sides of the paper, at the top, and at the bottom. If your letter is very short, you should make your margins larger.

CLOSING AND SIGNATURE: The closing is two spaces below the last line of the body. A comma follows it. Capitalize only the first word. Some common ways to close formal letters are:

Very truly yours,   Sincerely,
Yours truly,   Sincerely yours,

Sign the letter about one-half inch below the closing. Then type or print your name under your signature.

B. Put the following information in the correct place in the letter form on the next page. Add commas where necessary.

Customer Service Department, Sullivan Office Furniture
Company, 1432 Bradley Boulevard, Muskegon, Michigan 49441
July 12, 19XX
Dear Sir:
157 John Street, New York, New York 10038

Yours sincerely
Jane Fulton
Jane Fulton
Office Manager

_____

_____

_____

_____

_____

_____

_____

_____

XXXXXXXXXXXXXXXXXXXXXXXXXXXXXXXXXXXXXXXXXXXXXXX
XXXXXXXXXXXXXXXXXXXXXXXXXXXXXXXXXXXXXXXXXXXXXXX

XXXXXXXXXXXXXXXXXXXXXXXXXXXXXXXXXXXXXXXXXXXXXXX

XXXXXXXXXXXXXXXXXXXXXXXXXXXXXXXXXXXXXXXXXXXXXXX

XXXXXXXXXXXXXXXXXXXXXXXXXXXXXXXXXXXXXXXXXXXXX
XXXXXXXXXXXXXXXXXXXXXXXXXXXXXXXXXXXXXXXXXXXXXXX

_____

_____

_____

PART THREE

WRITING AND EDITING

Writing the First Draft

Now write your letter of complaint.

Editing Practice

Edit this letter twice and rewrite it correctly. The first time, check to see if the writer has used correct business letter form. Then check to see if the writer included all the necessary details, if he should take out some of the details, and if he has used polite, formal language. Make any other changes you think are necessary.

February 24, 19XX

125 South Street
Brattleboro
Vermont 05301

David Drew
Manager Repair Dept.
Empire Typewriter
Company
309 Fourth St,
Pipe Creek, Texas 78063

dear manager

last month I sent my typewriter to you for repairs because it wasn't working correctly. I got it for my birthday. You repair department promise to send to me in two weeks. I still haven't gotten it back. I need my typewriter now. You had better tell them to repair it and send it to me quickly.

David Wright

Editing Your Writing

Now look at your letter. Check it for:

1. Content

   Did you explain the problem clearly?

2. Organization

   a. Did you include all the necessary details?
   b. Did you include any unnecessary details?

3. Cohesion and style

   a. Did you use formal language?
   b. Did you use polite language?

Writing the Second Draft

A. After you edit your letter the first time, rewrite it neatly. Use good handwriting and correct form. Then check it for:

1. Grammar

   a. Did you use correct verb forms?
   b. Did you use past participles as adjectives correctly?

2. Form

   Did you use the correct business letter format, with a date, inside address, salutation, and closing?

B. Discuss the corrections you made with other students.

PART FOUR

COMMUNICATING THROUGH WRITING

Give your paragraph to your teacher for comments.

Sharing

Exchange letters with another student. Pretend you are the person who received the letter and decide what you will do about the complaint. Discuss your decision with the writer.

Using Feedback

Look at your teacher's comments. If you don't understand something, ask about it.

Developing Your Skills

Write a formal letter complaining about a problem at your school. It might be the courses the school offers, the cafeteria food, the lack of parking spaces, or anything else. Before you write your letter, find out the correct name and title of the person your letter should go to. For example, you might write to the cafeteria manager about a problem with the food. Share your letter with your classmates.

Developing Fluency

A. Write an informal letter to a friend at home complaining about something you don't like about the United States or Canada.

B. Write in your journal for twenty minutes about the most important thing(s) you have learned about writing in English since you started this course.

APPENDICES

APPENDIX 1

Spelling Rules for Adding Endings

Rules for Adding Endings That Begin with Vowels (*-ed, -ing, -er, -est*)

1. For words ending in a silent *e*, drop the *e* and add the ending.

    like → lik**ed**   make → mak**ing**   safe → saf**er**   fine → fin**est**

2. For one-syllable words ending in a single vowel and a single consonant, double the final consonant.

    bat → ba**tted**   run → ru**nning**   fat → fa**tter**   hot → ho**ttest**

3. Don't double the final consonant when the word has two final consonants or two vowels before a final consonant.

   pick → pick**ed**   sing → sing**ing**   clean → clean**er**   cool → cool**est**

4. For words of two or more syllables that end in a single vowel and a single consonant, double the final consonant if the word is accented on the final syllable.

   refer´ → refer**red**   begin´ → begin**ning**

5. For words of two or more syllables that end in a single vowel and a single consonant, make no change if the word isn't accented on the final syllable.

   trável → travel**ed**   fócus → focus**ed**

6. For words ending in a consonant and *y*, change the *y* to *i* and add the ending unless the ending begins with *i*.

   study → stud**ied**   dirty → dirt**ier**   sunny → sunn**iest**
   study → study**ing**   hurry → hurry**ing**

7. For words ending in a vowel and *y*, make no change before adding the ending.

   play → play**ed**   stay → stay**ing**

Rules for Adding Endings That Begin with Consonants (*ly, ment*)

8. For words ending in a silent *e*, make no change when adding endings that begin with consonants.

   fine → fine**ly**   state → state**ment**

9. For words ending in a consonant and *y*, change the *y* to *i* before adding the ending.

   happy → happ**ily**   merry → merr**iment**

Rules for Adding a Final *s* to Nouns and Verbs

10. Generally, add the *s* without making changes.

    sit → sit**s**   dance → dance**s**   play → play**s**   book → book**s**

11. If a word ends in a consonant and *y*, change the *y* to *i* and add *es*.

    marry → marr**ies**   study → stud**ies**   cherry → cherr**ies**

12. If a word ends in *ch, s, sh, x,* or *z*, add *es*.

    church → church**es**   cash → cash**es**   fizz → fizz**es**
    boss → boss**es**   mix → mix**es**

13. For words ending in *o*, sometimes add *es* and sometimes add *s*.

    tomato → tomato**es**   potato → potato**es**
    piano → piano**s**   radio → radio**s**

14. For words ending in *f* or *fe,* generally drop the *f* or *fe* and add *ves.*

knife → kni**ves**	wife → wi**ves**	life → li**ves**	loaf → loa**ves**
Exceptions:	safe → safe**s**	puff → puff**s**	roof → roof**s**

APPENDIX 2

Capitalization Rules

First Words

1. Capitalize the first word of every sentence.

    They live in Rome.   **Who** is it?

2. Capitalize the first word of a quotation.

    He said, "**My** name is Paul."   Jenny asked, "**When** is the party?"

Personal Names

3. Capitalize the names of people including initials and titles of address.

    Mrs. Jones   Mohandas Gandhi   John F. Kennedy

4. Capitalize family words if they appear alone or followed by a name.

    Let's go, **Dad.**   Where's **Grandma?**   She's at **Aunt Lucy's.**

5. Don't capitalize family words if they appear with a possessive pronoun or article.

    my **uncle**   her **mother**   our **grandparents**   an **aunt**

6. Capitalize the pronoun *I.*

    I have a book.   She's bigger than **I** am.

7. Capitalize names of God.

    God   Allah   Jesus Christ

8. Capitalize the names of nationalities, races, peoples, and religions.

    Japanese   Arab   Asian   Chicano   Muslim

9. Generally, don't capitalize occupations.

    I am a **secretary.**   She wants to be a **lawyer.**

Place Names

10. Capitalize the names of countries, states, provinces, and cities.

    Mexico **New York** **Ontario** **Tokyo**

11. Capitalize the names of oceans, lakes, rivers, islands, and mountains.

    the Atlantic Ocean **Lake Como** **the Amazon**
    Belle Isle **Mt. Everest**

12. Capitalize the names of geographical areas.

    the South **the East Coast** **Asia** **Antarctica**

13. Don't capitalize directions if they aren't names of geographical areas.

    He lives east of Toronto. **They traveled southwest.**

14. Capitalize names of schools, parks, buildings, and streets.

    the University **Central Park** **the Sears Building** **Oxford Road**
    of Georgia

Time Words

15. Capitalize names of days and months.

    Monday **Friday** **January** **March**

16. Capitalize names of holidays and historical events.

    Christmas **New Year's Day** **Independence Day** **World War II**

17. Don't capitalize names of seasons.

    spring **summer** *fall* **winter**

Titles

18. Capitalize the first word and all important words of titles of books, magazines, newspapers, and articles.

    Interactions *Newsweek*
    The New York Times "Rock Music Today"

19. Capitalize the first word and all important words of names of movies, plays, radio programs, and television programs.

    The African Queen *The Tempest* "News Roundup" "Fame"

20. Don't capitalize articles (*a, an, the*), conjunctions (*but, and, or*), and short prepositions (*of, with, in, on, for*) unless they are the first word of a title.

    The Life of Thomas Edison **War and Peace** **Death of a Salesman**

Names of Organizations

21. Capitalize the names of organizations, government groups, and businesses.

    International Student Association   the Senate   Gestetner

22. Capitalize trade names, but do not capitalize the name of the product.

    IBM typewriter   **Toyota** hatchback   **Kellogg's** cereal

Other

23. Capitalize the names of languages.

    Spanish   Thai   French   Japanese

24. Don't capitalize school subjects unless they are the names of languages or are followed by a number.

    geometry   music   English   Arabic   Biology 306

APPENDIX 3

Punctuation Rules

Period

1. Use a period after a statement or command.

    We are studying English.   Open your books to Chapter 3.

2. Use a period after most abbreviations.

    Mr.   Ms.   Dr.   Ave.   etc.   U.S.
    Exceptions: UN   NATO   IBM   AIDS

3. Use a period after initials.

    H. G. Wells   Dr. H. R. Hammond

Question Mark

4. Use a question mark after (not before) questions.

    Where are you going?   Is he here yet?

5. In a direct quotation, the question mark goes before the quotation marks.

    He asked, "What's your name?"

Exclamation Point

6. Use an exclamation point after exclamatory sentences or phrases.

> I won the lottery!   Be quiet!   Wow!

Comma

7. Use a comma before a conjunction (*and, or, so, but*) that separates two independent clauses.

> She wanted to go to work, so she decided to take an English course.
> He wasn't happy in that apartment, but he didn't have the money to move.

8. Don't use a comma before a conjunction that separates two phrases that aren't complete sentences.

> She worked in the library and studied at night.
> Do you want to go to a movie or stay home?

9. Use a comma before an introductory clause or phrase (generally if it is five or more words long).

> After a beautiful wedding ceremony, they had a reception in her mother's home.
> If you want to write well, you should practice writing almost every night.

10. Use a comma to separate interrupting expressions from the rest of a sentence.

> Do you know, by the way, what time dinner is?
> Many of the students, I found out, stayed on campus during the summer.

11. Use a comma after transitional expressions.

> In addition, he stole all her jewelry.
> However, he left the TV.

Common transitional expressions are:

therefore	moreover	however
consequently	furthermore	nevertheless
for this reason	besides	on the other hand
also	in fact	for example
in addition	similarly	for instance

12. Use a comma to separate names of people in direct address from the rest of a sentence.

> Jane, have you seen Paul?
> We aren't sure, Mrs. Shapiro, where he is.

13. Use a comma after *yes* and *no* in answers.

> Yes, he was here a minute ago.
> No, I haven't.

14. Use a comma to separate items in a series.

> We have coffee, tea, and milk.
> He looked in the refrigerator, on the shelves, and in the cupboard.

15. Use a comma to separate an appositive from the rest of a sentence.

> Mrs. Sampson, his English teacher, gave him a good recommendation.
> Would you like to try a taco, a delicious Mexican food?

16. If a date or address has two or more parts, use a comma after each part.

> I was born on June 5, 1968.
> The house at 230 Seventh Street, Miami, Florida, is for sale.

17. Use a comma to separate contrasting information from the rest of the sentence.

> It wasn't Maria, but Parvin, who was absent.
> Bring your writing book, not your reading book.

18. Use a comma to separate quotations from the rest of a sentence.

> He asked, "What are we going to do?"
> "I'm working downtown," he said.

19. Use a comma to separate two or more adjectives that each modify the noun alone.

> She was an intelligent, beautiful actress. (*intelligent* and *beautiful* actress)
> Eat those delicious green beans. (*delicious* modifies *green beans*)

20. Use a comma to separate nonrestrictive clauses from the rest of a sentence. A nonrestrictive clause gives more information about the noun it describes, but it isn't needed to identify the noun. Clauses after proper names are nonrestrictive and require commas.

> *It's a Wonderful Life,* which is often on television at Christmastime, is my favorite movie.
> James Stewart, who plays a man thinking of killing himself, is the star of *It's a Wonderful Life.*

Quotation Marks

21. Use quotation marks at the beginning and end of exact quotations. Other punctuation marks go before the end quotation marks.

> He said, "I'm going to Montreal."
> "How are you?" he asked.

22. Use quotation marks before and after titles of stories, articles, songs, and television programs. Periods and commas go before the final quotation marks, while question marks and exclamation points normally go after them.

> Do you like to watch "Dallas" on television?
> My favorite song is "Let It Be."
> Do you like the story "Gift of the Magi"?

Apostrophes

23. Use apostrophes in contractions.

>   don't   it's   we've   they're

24. Use an apostrophe to make possessive nouns.

>   *Singular:*   Jerry's   my boss's
>   *Plural:*   the children's   the Smiths'

Underlining

25. Underline the titles of books, magazines, newspapers, plays, and movies.

>   I am reading <u>One Hundred Years of Solitude.</u>
>   Did you like the movie <u>The Wizard of Oz</u>?

CHAPTER 1 FEEDBACK SHEET

Student Name _____ Date _____

Personal reaction:

_____

_____

_____

_____

_____

Chapter checklist:

	Good	Needs Work
Content		
Level of interest of information	☐	☐
Organization		
1. All information about one person	☐	☐
2. Order of sentences	☐	☐
3. Topic sentence	☐	☐
Cohesion and Style		
1. Connecting sentences with *and, so, but*	☐	☐
2. Use of *also*	☐	☐
Grammar		
1. Present tense verbs	☐	☐
2. Pronouns	☐	☐
Form		
1. Paragraph form	☐	☐
2. Spelling	☐	☐
3. Handwriting	☐	☐

Other comments:

_____

_____

_____

_____

_____

CHAPTER 2 FEEDBACK SHEET

Student Name _____ Date _____

Personal reaction:

_____

_____

_____

_____

_____

Chapter checklist:

	Good	Needs Work
Content		
Use of interesting adjectives	☐	☐
Organization		
1. General to specific	☐	☐
2. Order of sentences	☐	☐
Cohesion and Style		
1. Connecting sentences	☐	☐
2. Use of pronouns	☐	☐
3. Placement of adjectives	☐	☐
4. Use of prepositional phrases	☐	☐
Grammar		
1. Subject-verb agreement	☐	☐
2. Use of *a/an* and *the*	☐	☐
Form		
1. Paragraph form	☐	☐
2. Spelling of present participles	☐	☐

Other comments:

_____

_____

_____

_____

_____

CHAPTER 3 FEEDBACK SHEET

Student Name _____ Date _____

Personal reaction:

_____

_____

_____

_____

_____

Chapter checklist:

	Good	Needs Work
Content		
1. Interesting information	☐	☐
2. Clear information	☐	☐
Organization		
1. Topic sentence	☐	☐
2. All information about the holiday	☐	☐
3. Order of sentences	☐	☐
Cohesion and Style		
1. Connecting sentences	☐	☐
2. Use of appositives	☐	☐
3. Use of *such as*		
Grammar		
1. Present-tense verbs	☐	☐
2. Count and noncount nouns	☐	☐
Form		
1. Paragraph form	☐	☐
2. Spelling of words with *-s* endings	☐	☐
3. Commas with appositives	☐	☐

Other comments:

_____

_____

_____

_____

_____

CHAPTER 4 FEEDBACK SHEET

Student Name _____ Date _____

Personal reaction:

_____

_____

_____

_____

_____

Chapter checklist:

	Good	Needs Work
Content		
1. Interesting activities	☐	☐
2. Clear directions	☐	☐
Organization		
Each paragraph about a different topic	☐	☐
Cohesion and Style		
1. Prepositions	☐	☐
2. Use of *there* and *it*	☐	☐
Grammar		
1. Verb forms	☐	☐
2. Subject-verb agreement	☐	☐
Form		
1. Date	☐	☐
2. Salutation	☐	☐
3. Indentation of paragraphs	☐	☐
4. Closing	☐	☐

Other comments:

_____

_____

_____

_____

_____

CHAPTER 5 FEEDBACK SHEET

Student Name _____ Date _____

Personal reaction:

_____

_____

_____

_____

_____

Chapter checklist:

	Good	Needs Work
Content		
1. Interesting information	☐	☐
2. Important information	☐	☐
3. Interesting title	☐	☐
Organization		
1. Topic sentence	☐	☐
2. All sentences about one topic	☐	☐
3. Order of sentences	☐	☐
Cohesion and Style		
1. Combining sentences with time words	☐	☐
2. Combining sentences with *and, but, so,* and *because*	☐	☐
Grammar		
1. Nouns	☐	☐
2. Pronouns	☐	☐
3. Articles	☐	☐
4. Sentence structure (no fragments)	☐	☐
5. Past-tense verbs	☐	☐
Form		
1. Paragraph form	☐	☐
2. Capitalization of title	☐	☐
3. Punctuation with combined sentences	☐	☐

Other comments:

_____

_____

_____

_____

_____

CHAPTER 6 FEEDBACK SHEET

Student Name _____ Date _____

Personal reaction:

_____

_____

_____

_____

_____

Chapter checklist:

	Good	Needs Work
Content		
1. Clear story	☐	☐
2. Important information	☐	☐
Organization		
1. Use of time words	☐	☐
2. Title	☐	☐
Cohesion and Style		
1. Varied time expressions	☐	☐
2. Descriptions	☐	☐
3. Quotations	☐	☐
Grammar		
1. Past-tense verbs	☐	☐
2. Present-continuous tense verbs	☐	☐
3. Sentence structure (no fragments)	☐	☐
Form		
1. Use of commas	☐	☐
2. Use of quotation marks	☐	☐

Other comments:

_____

_____

_____

_____

_____

CHAPTER 7 FEEDBACK SHEET

Student Name _____ Date _____

Personal reaction:

_____

_____

_____

_____

Chapter checklist:

	Good	Needs Work
Content		
1. Interesting information	☐	☐
2. Reasons and examples	☐	☐
Organization		
1. Topic sentence	☐	☐
2. All information about one topic	☐	☐
Cohesion and Style		
1. Use of synonyms	☐	☐
2. Relative clauses	☐	☐
3. Use of *in addition, for example,* and *however*	☐	☐
Grammar		
1. Use of noun forms	☐	☐
2. Use of verb forms	☐	☐
Form		
Use of commas	☐	☐

Other comments:

_____

_____

_____

_____

CHAPTER 8 FEEDBACK SHEET

Student Name _____ Date _____

Personal reaction:

_____

_____

_____

_____

_____

Chapter checklist:

	Good	Needs Work
Content		
1. Interesting title	☐	☐
2. Interesting information	☐	☐
3. Clear presentation	☐	☐
Organization		
1. Use of details	☐	☐
2. Topic sentence	☐	☐
3. Concluding sentence	☐	☐
Cohesion and Style		
Use of appositives	☐	☐
Grammar		
1. Verb tenses/historical present	☐	☐
2. Sentence structure (no fragments)	☐	☐
Form		
1. Capitalization of title	☐	☐
2. Use of commas	☐	☐

Other comments:

_____

_____

_____

_____

_____

CHAPTER 9 FEEDBACK SHEET

Student Name _____ Date _____

Personal reaction:

_____

_____

_____

_____

_____

Chapter checklist:

	Good	Needs Work
Content		
1. Interesting information	☐	☐
2. Important information	☐	☐
Organization		
1. Topic sentence	☐	☐
2. Well-organized sentences	☐	☐
3. Concluding sentence	☐	☐
Cohesion and Style		
1. Use of *however, also, in addition,* and *in fact*	☐	☐
2. Use of *so that*	☐	☐
3. Use of long forms rather than contractions	☐	☐
Grammar		
Verb forms	☐	☐
Form		
1. Use of commas	☐	☐
2. Spelling of verb forms	☐	☐
3. Capitalization	☐	☐

Other comments:

_____

_____

_____

_____

_____

CHAPTER 10 FEEDBACK SHEET

Student Name _____ Date _____

Personal reaction:

_____

_____

_____

_____

_____

Chapter checklist:

	Good	Needs Work
Content		
1. Interesting information	☐	☐
2. Enough information	☐	☐
Organization		
1. Order of information	☐	☐
2. Consistent type of information	☐	☐
Cohesion and Style		
1. Use of *in addition to, besides, another, the first (second,* etc.)	☐	☐
2. Use of quantifiers	☐	☐
3. Use of pronouns and pronominal expressions	☐	☐
4. Use of relative clauses	☐	☐
Grammar		
1. Verb forms	☐	☐
2. Sentence structure (no fragments)	☐	☐
Form		
Use of commas with nonrestrictive relative clauses	☐	☐

Other comments:

_____

_____

_____

_____

_____

CHAPTER 11 FEEDBACK SHEET

Student Name _____ Date _____

Personal reaction:

_____

_____

_____

_____

_____

Chapter checklist:

	Good	Needs Work
Content		
1. Interesting information	☐	☐
2. Use of reasons	☐	☐
Organization		
1. Complete information	☐	☐
2. Topic sentence	☐	☐
Cohesion and Style		
1. Use of *it* and *this*	☐	☐
2. Use of *you* for people in general	☐	☐
Grammar		
1. Use of adjectives + infinitive complements	☐	☐
2. Use of gerunds	☐	☐
Form		
Superlative forms	☐	☐

Other comments:

_____

_____

_____

_____

_____

CHAPTER 12 FEEDBACK SHEET

Student Name _____ Date _____

Personal reaction:

_____

_____

_____

_____

_____

Chapter checklist:

	Good	Needs Work
Content		
Clear presentation of information	☐	☐
Organization		
1. Necessary detail	☐	☐
2. All information about the topic	☐	☐
Cohesion and Style		
1. Use of formal language	☐	☐
2. Polite tone	☐	☐
Grammar		
1. Verb forms	☐	☐
2. Past participles as adjectives	☐	☐
Form		
Correct format (date, inside address, salutation, and closing)	☐	☐

Other comments:

_____

_____

_____

_____

_____